Godey's Lady's Book, Vol. 42, January, 1851

by Various

ISBN: 9781318811496

Copyright © 2016 by HardPress

HardPress
8345 NW 66TH ST #2561
MIAMI FL 33166-2626
USA
Email: info@hardpress.net

Ordering Information:

Quantity sales. Special discounts are available on quantity purchases by corporations, associations, and others. For details, contact the publisher by email at the address above.

Printed in the United States of America, United Kingdom and Australia

NEW YEAR'S DAY IN FRANCE.

MODEL COTTAGE.

A Cottage in the Style of Heriot's Hospital, Edinburgh.

The elevation is shown in fig. 1, the ground-plan in fig. 2.

Accommodation.—The plan shows a porch, *a*; a lobby, *b*; living room, *c*; kitchen, *d*; back-kitchen, *e*; pantry, *f*; dairy, *g*; bed-closet, *h*; store-closet, *i*; fuel, *k*; cow-house, *l*; pig-stye, *m*; yard, *n*; dust-hole, *q*.

The Scotch are great admirers of this style, as belonging to one of their favorite public buildings, which is said to have been designed by the celebrated Inigo Jones. The style is that of the times of Queen Elizabeth, and King James VI. of Scotland and I. of England.

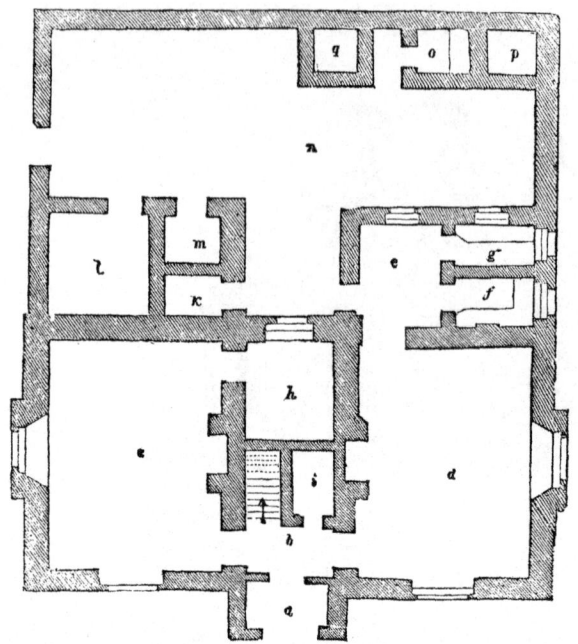

GODEY'S LADY'S BOOK.

PHILADELPHIA, JANUARY, 1851.

THE CONSTANT; OR, THE ANNIVERSARY PRESENT.

BY ALICE B. NEAL.

(*See Plate.*)

It has an excellent influence on one's moral health to meet now and then in society, or, better still, in the close communion of home life, such a woman as Catherine Grant. She influences every one that comes within the pure atmosphere of her friendship, and as unconsciously to them as to herself. She never moralizes, or commands reform. There is no parade of her individual principle in any way, but she always *acts* rightly; and, if her opinion is called forth, it is given promptly and quietly, but very firmly.

Yet, though even strangers say this of her now, there was a time when few suspected the moral strength of her character. Not that principle was wanting; but it had never been called forth. She moved in her own circle with very little remark or comment. She was cheerful, and even sprightly in her manner, and her large blue eyes, as well as her lips, always spoke the truth. I do not know that she was ever called beautiful; but there was an air of *ladyhood* about her, from the folding of her soft brown hair to the gloving of a somewhat large but exquisitely-shaped hand, that marked her at once as possessing both taste and refinement.

I remember that friends spoke of her engagement with Willis Grant as a "good match," and rather wondered that she did not seem more elated with the prospect of being the mistress of such a pleasant little establishment as would be hers, for she was one of a large family of daughters, and her father's income as a professional man did not equal that of Willis, who was at the head of one of our largest mercantile houses. But it was in her nature to take things calmly, though she was young, and all the kindness of his attentions, and the prospect of a new home, as much as any happy bride could have done. It *was* a delightful home—not so extravagantly furnished as Willis would have chosen it to be, but tasteful, and withal including many of those luxuries and elegancies which we of the nineteenth century are rapidly, too rapidly, learning to need. Willis declared that no one could be happier than they were; and, strange as it may seem, the envious world for once prophesied no cloud in the future.

But we have nothing to do with that first eventful year of married life—the year of attrition in mind and character, when two natures, differing in many points, and these sharpened as it were by education, are suddenly brought into immediate contact. There were some ideals overthrown, no doubt—it is often so; and some good qualities discovered, which were unsuspected before. The second anniversary of the wedding-day was also the birth-day of a darling child, and the home was more homelike than ever.

Yet Willis Grant was seldom there. It was not that he loved his wife the less—that her beauty had faded, or her temper changed. She was the same as ever—gentle, affectionate, and thoughtful for his wishes; and he appreciated all this. But before he had known her, in those wild idle days of early manhood, when the spirit craves continual excitement, and has not yet learned that it is the love of woman's purer nature which it needs, Willis had chosen his associates in a circle which it was very difficult to break from, now that their society was no longer essential to him. He was close in his attention to business; his great, success had arisen from industry as well as talent; but when the counting-house was closed, there was no family circle to welcome him, and the doors of the club-house were invitingly open.

True, it was one of the most respectable clubs of the city, mostly composed of young business men like himself, who discussed the tariffs and their effects upon trade over their *recherche* dinners, and chatted of European politics over their wine. And this reminds us of one thing that argues much, if not more than anything else, against the club-house system, that is so rapidly gaining favor in our cities. It accustoms the young man just entering life to a surrounding of luxury that he cannot himself consistently support when he begins to think of having a home of his own. He passes his evenings in a beautiful saloon, where the light is brilliant, yet tempered; where crimson curtains and a blazing fire speak at once of comfort and affluence of means. There are no discomforts, such as any one meets with more or less, inevitably, in private families—nothing to jar upon the spirit of self-indulgence and indolence which is thus fostered. The dinners, in cooking and service, are unexceptionable; and there are always plenty of associates as idle and thoughtless, and as good-natured, as himself, to make a jest of domestic life and domestic virtues. And, by-and-by, there is a stronger stimulus wanted, and the jest becomes more wanton over the roulette table or the keenly contested rubber; and the wine circulates more freely as the fire of youth goes out and leaves the ashes of mental and moral desolation. Ah no! the club-house is no conservator of the purity of social life, and this Catherine Grant soon felt, as night after night her husband left her to the society of her own thoughts, or her favorite books, to meet old friends in its familiar saloons, and show them that he at least was none the less "a good fellow" for being a married man!

It was all very well, no doubt, to be able to break away from the pleasant parlor, and the interesting woman who was the presiding genius of his household, and spend his evenings in the society of gay gallants who talked of horses and Tedesco's figure, or the gray-headed votaries of the whist table, who played the game as if the presidency depended upon "following lead," and each trump was a diamond of inestimable worth, to be cherished and reserved, and parted with only at the last extremity. Sometimes a thought of comparison would arise, as he sat with elevated feet beside the anthracite fire, and gazed steadfastly on his patent leathers. Sometimes the idle jests and the heartless laughter would jar upon his ear; and the cigar was suffered to die out as, in thoughts of wife and child, he forgot to put it to his lips. But the injustice of his conduct, in thus depriving them of his society, did not once cross his mind, until he was involuntarily made the witness of a visit between

Catherine and a lady who had been her intimate friend before marriage.

He had returned hurriedly one morning in search of some papers left in his own room, dignified by the name of study, though it must be confessed that he passed but little time there. It communicated with Catherine's apartment, which was just then occupied by the two ladies in confidential chat.

"And so you won't go to Mrs Sawyer's to-night?" said Miss Lyons, who had thrown herself at full length upon a couch, and was idly teazing the baby with the tassel of her muff. "How provoking you are! You might as well be dead as married! It's well for your husband that I'm not in your place. Why, every one's talking about it, my child, how you are cooped up here, and Willis at the club-house night after night. Morgan told me he was always there, and asked me what kind of a wife he had—whether you quarreled or flirted, that he was away from you so much."

Had the heedless speaker glanced up from her play with little Gertrude, she would have seen her friend's face suffused with a slight flush, for the last was a view of the case entirely new to her. But she said, quietly as ever—

"'Everybody' might be in better business, Nell; and why is it well for Willis that you are not in my place?"

"Why? Because I'd pay him in his own coin; he should not have the game all in his own hands. If he went to the club, I'd flirt, that's all, and we'd see who would hold out the longer."

"Bad principle, Nelly. 'Two wrongs,' as the old proverb says, 'never make a right;' and yet I am sorry I said that, for so long as it gives Willis pleasure, and he is not drawn from his business by it, it is no wrong, though there is danger to any man in confirmed habits of 'good-fellowship,' as it is called. No one could see that more plainly than I do, or dread it more. Of course, when we love a person it is natural to wish to be with him as much as possible; and I must confess I am a little lonely now and then. But your plan would never succeed, nor would it be wise to annoy my husband with complaints. Nothing provokes a man like an expostulation."

"And what do you do, then?"

"Nothing at all but try to make his home as pleasant as possible, and when he is weary of his gay companions he will return to me with more interest."

"Well, well," broke in her visitor; "Morgan can make up his mind to a very different state of things. I shall stipulate, first of all, that he must give up that abominable club-house."

"And do you intend to lay your flirting propensities on the same altar of mutual happiness?"

Willis did not hear the reply, for he stole softly away, annoyed, as he thought, at having been a listener to what was not intended for his ears. But there was a little sting of self-reproach at his selfish desertion of home, and, more than all, that Catherine should have been blamed for offences that any one who had known her would never have attributed to her.

"Ah, by the way, Kate," he said that evening, turning suddenly, as she stood arranging her work-table beneath the gas light, "how about that invitation to Mrs. Sawyer's? It was for to-night, if I recollect?"

"I sent regrets, of course, as you expressed no wish to go; and, to tell the truth, I would much rather pass the evening quietly here with you. How long it is since we have had one of those nice old-fashioned chats! Not since baby has been my companion."

This was said in a cheerful tone, as a reminiscence, not as a reproach; and yet Willis felt the morning's uncomfortable sensations return, though he tried to dispel them by stooping to kiss her forehead. Nevertheless, he ordered his coat, as the servant came in to remove the tea things, and took up his gloves from the table. The very consciousness of being in the wrong prevented an acknowledgment, even by an act so simple as giving up one evening's engagement.

"And here she comes!" he said, as the nurse drew the cradle from an adjoining room, so lightly that the little creature did not move or stir in her sweet sleep. And when his wife threw back the light covering, and said, "*Isn't she beautiful*, Willis?" as only a young mother could say it, it must be confessed that he thought himself a very fortunate man to have two such treasures, and he could not help saying so.

"I love to have the little thing where I can watch her myself; so, when there is no one in, nurse spares her to me, and we sit here as cosily as possible. I could watch her for hours. Sometimes she does not move, and then she will smile so sweetly in her sleep—and only look at those dear little dimpled hands, Willis!"

And yet Willis took the coat when it came, though with a guilty feeling at heart. The greater the self-reproach, the more the pride that arose to combat it; and he drew on his gloves resolutely.

"Don't sit up for me," he said, as he had said a hundred times before; and in a moment the hall door shut with a clang, as he passed into the street. Catherine echoed the sound with a half sigh. The morning's conversation rose to her recollection, and she had hoped, she scarce knew why, that Willis would remain with her that evening. But she checked the regretful reverie, and took up the pretty little sock she was knitting for Gertrude, and soon became engrossed in counting and all the after mysteries of this truly feminine employment.

Willis was ill at ease. He met young Morgan on the steps, and returned his bow very coldly. His usual companions were absent, and, after haunting the saloon restlessly for an hour, he strolled down to his counting-house. He knew that the foreign correspondence had just arrived, and, as he expected, his confidential clerk was still at the desk. And here he found, much to his dismay, that the presence of one of the firm was immediately necessary in Paris, and that, as the partner who usually attended to this branch of the business was ill, the journey would devolve on him. He was detained until a late hour, and as he turned his steps homeward the scene that he had left there rose vividly to his mind. He hurried up the steps, hoping to find Catherine still there, but the room was empty, and the fire, glowing redly through the bars of the grate, was the only thing to welcome him. He stood a long time, leaning his elbow on the marble of the mantel, and thought over many things that had happened within the last few years—the many happy social evenings he had passed at that very hearth; the unvarying love and constancy of his wife; of his late neglect, for he could call it by no gentler name; and then came the thought that he must leave all this domestic peace, which he had valued so little—and who knew what might chance before he should return? He kissed his sleeping wife and child with unwonted tenderness, as he entered their apartment, and thought that they had never been so dear to him before.

It would be their first protracted separation, and Catherine was sad enough when its necessity was announced to her. But all preparations were hastened; and, at the close of the week, they were standing together in the dining-room, the last trunk locked, and the carriage waiting at the door that was to convey Willis to the steamer.

"And mind you do not get ill in my absence, Kate," he said, as he smoothed back her beautiful hair, and looked down fondly in her face. "If you are very good, as they tell children, I will send you the most charming present you can conceive of, or that Paris can offer, for the anniversary of our wedding-day. Too bad that we shall be separated, for the first time; but three months will soon pass away."

And Catherine smiled through the tears that were trembling in her eyes, at the half sad, half playful words; and a wifelike glance of trustfulness told how very dear he was.

There is nothing very romantic nowadays in a voyage to Europe. It has become a commonplace, everyday journey. You step to the deck of the steamer with less fear and trembling of friends than was once bestowed on a passage down the Hudson, and before you are fairly recovered from the first shock of sea-sickness, you have reached the destined port. But, for all that, longing eyes watch the rapid motion of the vessel as it lessens in the distance, and many a prayer is wafted to its white sails by the sighing night-wind. There are lonely hours to remind one that the broad and silent sea is rolling between us and those we love, and we know that it is sometimes treacherous in its tranquillity.

It is then we bless the quiet messengers that come from afar to tell us of their well-being—when, the seal, with its loving device, is pressed to trembling lips, and the well-known hand recalls the form of the absent one so vividly. So, at last, the long-looked-for letters came with tidings of the safe arrival of Mr. Grant at his destination, and the hope that his return would be more speedy than had been anticipated. A month passed slowly away, and little Gertrude had been her mother's best comforter in absence. Every day some new intelligence lighted her bright eyes, and Catherine could trace another token of resemblance to the absent one. But, suddenly, the child grew ill, and the pain of separation was augmented as day by day the mother watched over her alone.

It was her first experience of the illness of childhood, and it required all her strength and all her calmness to be patient, while sitting hour after hour with the moaning infant cradled in her arms, unable to understand or relieve its sufferings, and tortured by the dull look of apathy which alone answered to her fond or despairing exclamations. She had forgotten that the birthday of the infant was so near—that first birthday—and the anniversary which they had twice welcomed so joyfully. At last the crisis came; the long night closed in drearily, and the physician told her that, ere morning, there would be hope or despair. Those who have thus watched can alone understand the agony of that midnight vigil; how every breath was counted, and every flush marked with wild anxiety. And Catherine sat there, forgetting that food or rest was necessary to her, conscious only of the suffering of her child, and picturing darkly to herself the loneliness of the future, should it be taken from her. How could she survive the interval that would elapse before her husband's return?

and how dreary would be the meeting which she had hitherto anticipated with so much pleasure!

She was not to be so sorely tried. The hard feverish pulse gave place to a gentler beating; the fever flush passed away; and the regular heaving of a quiet sleep gave token at length that all danger to the child was over.

Then, for the first time, Catherine was persuaded to seek rest for herself, and all her anxiety was forgotten in a deep and trance-like slumber.

When she awoke there were letters and packages lying beside her bed, directed by her husband; and after she had once more assured herself that it was no dream the child was really safe, she opened them eagerly. The letter announced that the business was happily adjusted, and that his return might be looked for by the next steamer. Meantime, he said, he had sent some things to amuse her, and more particularly the choice gift for the anniversary of their marriage. It was the morning of that very day! She had not thought of it before. She stooped to place a birthday kiss upon the fair but wasted little face beside her, and then tore open the envelops. There were many beautiful things, "such as ladies love to look upon," and at the last she came to a small package marked, "*For our wedding day*." It contained a little jewel case; but there was nothing on the snowy satin cushion but a pair of daintily wrought clasps for the robe of the little child, marked, "with a father's love;" and then, as she was replacing them, a sealed envelop caught her eye. There was an inclosure directed to a name she was not familiar with, and a few lines penciled for herself:—

"DEAR KATE: I have searched all over Paris, and could not find anything that I thought would please you better than the inclosed, which is my resignation of club membership. Will you please send it to the president, and accept the true and earnest love of   YOUR ABSENT HUSBAND."

Then he had not been unmindful of her silent regret; he still loved his home, and the dangerous hour of his temptation was passed! Had she not great reason for the gush of love and thankfulness that filled her heart and renewed her strength that happy morning—her child saved, and her husband, as it were, restored to her? Ere he came, the little one was fast regaining her bright playfulness, and became a stronger tie between Willis Grant and his happy home. I do not know that you and I, dear reader, would have learned the secret of his renewed devotion to his wife, had he not told Nelly Lyons himself that "Kate's way was the best, and she had better try it with Morgan, if ever he showed an undue fondness for the club after their marriage." Of course, the volatile girl could not help telling the story, and when two know a thing, as we are all aware, it is a secret no longer.

A PARABLE.

BY JAMES CARRUTHERS.

"It is a marvel," remarked the youth Silas to his companion, "that, after so many years of unremitting application, favored by the combination of extraordinary advantages, I should yet have accomplished nothing. Scholarly toil, indeed, is not without its meet reward. But in much wisdom is much grief, when it serves not to advance the well-being of its possessor."

"I have remarked, as thou hast," returned the companion of Silas, "how sorely thou hast been distanced in thy life's pursuit by those who came after with far less ability and fewer advantages; and, if thou wilt believe me, have read the marvel. Last noon, while in attendance on the Syrian race, I observed that the untamed, high-mettled steed, that, in his daring strength and almost limitless swiftness, scorned his rider's curb, though traveling a space far more extended than the appointed course, and, surmounting every hill, left the race to be won by the well-governed courser that obeyed the rein, and, in the track marked out for his progress, reached the goal."

ERAS OF LIFE.

BY MRS. A.F. LAW

(*See Plate.*)

BAPTISM

"We receive this child into the congregation of Christ's flock, and do sign her with the sign of the cross—in token that hereafter she shall not be ashamed to confess the faith of Christ crucified, and manfully fight under his banner against sin, the world, and the devil; and to continue Christ's faithful soldier and servant, unto her life's end."—BAPTISMAL SERVICE OF P.E.C.

In the house of prayer we enter, through its aisles our course we wend,

And before the sacred altar on our knees we humbly bend;

Craving, for a young immortal, God's beneficence and grace,

That, through Christ's unfailing succor, she may win the victor race.

Water from *baptismal fountain* rests on a "young soldier," sworn

By the cross' holy signet to defend the "Virgin-born."

May she never faint or falter in the raging war of sin,

And, encased in Faith's tried armor, a triumphant conquest win!

To the Triune One our darling trustingly we now commend,

And for full and *free* salvation, from our hearts pure thanks ascend.

COMMUNION.

"Hail! sacred feast, which Jesus makes—

Rich banquet of his flesh and blood:

Thrice happy he who here partakes

That sacred stream, that heavenly food."

With a bearing meekly grateful, slow approach the *sacred feast*,
And, with penitential gladness, take, by faith, this Eucharist.
Hark! how sweetly, o'er it stealing, come the sounds of pardoning love!
Winning back to paths of virtue all who now in error rove.
Here is food for all who languish, and for those who, fainting, thirst—
Free, from Christ, the *Living Fountain*, crystal waters ceaseless burst!
Come, ye sad and weary-hearted, bending 'neath a weight of woe—
Here the *Comforter* is waiting his rich blessings to bestow!
None need linger—*all* are bidden to this "Supper of the Lamb:"
Come, and by this outward token, worship God, the great "I AM!"

MARRIAGE

"One sacred oath hath tied

Our loves; one destiny our life shall guide;

Nor wild nor deep our common way divide!"

Choral voices float around us, music on the night air swells;

Hill and dell resound with echoes of the gleeful wedding bells!

Ushered thus, we haste to enter on a scene of radiant joy—

List'ning vows in ardor plighted, which alone can death destroy.

Passing fair the bride appeareth, in her robes of snowy white,

While the veil around her streameth, like a silvery halo's light;

And amid her hair's rich braidings rests the pearly orange bough,

With its fragrant blossoms pressing on her pure, unclouded brow.

Love's devotion yields the future with young Hope's resplendent beam;

And her spirit thrills with rapture, yielding to its blissful dream!

DEATH.

"Death, thou art infinite!"

"All that live must die,

Passing through nature to Eternity."

Now we chant a miserere which proclaims the *end of man*—

Telling, in prophetic language, "*Life,*" at best, "*is but a span!*"

Scarcely treading, slowly enter, reverently bend the knee—

List the Spirit's inward whisper, and from *worldly thoughts* be free.

Here we view a weary pilgrim, cradled in a dreamless sleep;

Human sounds no more shall reach her, for its spell is "long and deep!"

Gaze upon the marble features! Mark how peacefully they rest!

Anguished thought, and sorrow's heavings, all are parted from that breast!

Soon on mother earth reposing, this cold form shall calmly lie,

Till, by God's dread trump awakened, it shall mount to realms on high.

FOUR SONNETS TO THE FOUR SEASONS.

BY MARY SPENSER PEASE.

(*See Plate.*)

SPRING.

From mountain top, and from the deep-voiced valley,

The snow-white mists are slowly upward wreathing:

Now floating wide, now hovering close, to dally

With sportive winds, around them lightly breathing,

Till, in the quickening Spring-shine through them creeping,

Their gloomy power dissolves in warmth and gladness;

While swift, new tides through Nature's heart-pulse sweeping.

Floods all her veins with a delicious madness.

Warmed into life, a world of bright shapes thronging—

Young, tender leaf-buds in fresh greenness swelling,

Flower, bird, and insect, with prophetic longing,

Pour forth their joy in tremulous hymns upwelling:

Thus, Love's Spring sun dispels all chill and sorrow

With joyful promise of Love's fullest morrow.

SUMMER.

Sweet incense from the heart of myriad flowers,

Sweet as the breath that parts the lips of love,

Floats softly upward through the sunny hours,

Hiving its fragrance in the warmth above:

Big with rich store, the teeming earth yields up

The increase of her harvest treasury;

While golden wine, from Nature's brimming cup,

Quickens her pulse to love-toned melody.

Full choiréd praise from countless glad throats break,

More dazzling bright doth gleam night's dewy eyes;

A newer witchery doth the great moon wake;

More mellow languisheth the bending skies:

Thus, through the heart Life's Summer-sun comes stealing,

Spring's wildest promise in Love's fulness sealing.

AUTUMN.

Athwart the ripe, red sunshine fitfully,

Like withering doubts through Love's warm, flushing breast,

With wailing voice of saddest augury,

Sweeps from the frozen North a phantom guest.

With icy finger on each yellow leaf

Writes he the history of the dying year.

Love's harvest reaped, the grainless stalk and sheaf—

Like plundered hearts, unkerneled of sweet cheer—

Lie black and bare, exposed to rudest tread:

While still, with semblance of the Summer brave,

Soft, pitying airs float o'er its cold death-bed;

Bright flowers and motley leaves flaunt o'er its grave:

As in Earth's Autumn—so, through weeping showers,

Love sighs a mournful requiem over bygone hours.

WINTER.

Locked in a close embrace, like that of Death,

Earth's pulseless heart reposes, mute and chill;

Within her frozen breast, her frozen breath,

In its forgotten fragrance, slumbereth still:

Sapless her veins, and numb her withered arms,

That still, outstretched, stand grim mementos drear

Of her once gorgeous and full-leavéd charms.

Of flower and fruit, all increase of the year:

Voiceless the river, in ice fretwork chained;

Hushed the sweet cadences of bird and bee;

Dumb the last echo to soft music trained,

And warmth and life are a past memory:

Thus, buried deep within dull Winter's rime,

Love dreamless sleeps through the long Winter-time.

LIFE IN THE WOODS.—A SONG.

BY GEO. P. MORRIS.

A merry life does the hunter lead!

He wakes with the dawn of day;

He whistles his dog—he mounts his steed,

And sends to the woods away!

The lightsome tramp of the deer he'll mark,

As they troop in herds along;

And his rifle startles the cheerful lark,

As she carols his morning song.

The hunter's life is the life for me!

That is the life for a man!

Let others sing of a home on the sea,

But match me the woods if you can.

Then give me a gun—I've an eye to mark

The deer, as they bound along!

My steed, dog, and gun, and the cheerful lark,

To carol my morning song.

THE SYLPHS OF THE SEASONS

WHAT IS LIFE?

BY MARY M. CHASE.

One sunshiny afternoon, a little girl sat in a wood playing with moss and stones. She was a pretty child; but there was a wishful, earnest look in her eye, at times, that made people say, "She is a good little girl; but she won't live long." But she did not think of that to-day, for a fine western wind was shaking the branches merrily above her head, and a family of young rabbits that lived near by kept peeping out to watch her motions. She threw bread to the rabbits from the pockets of her apron, and laughed to see them eat. She laughed, also, to hear the wild, boisterous wind shouting among the leaves, and then she sang parts of a song that she had imperfectly learned—

"Hurrah for the oak! for the brave old oak,

That hath ruled in the greenwood long!"

and the louder the wind roared, the louder she sang. Presently, a light-winged seed swept by her; she reached out her pretty hand and caught it. It was an ugly brown seed; but she said, as she looked at it—

"Mother says, if I plant a seed, may be it will grow to be a tree. So I will see."

Then she scraped away a little of the mellow earth, and put the seed safely down, and covered it again. She made a little paling around the spot With dry sticks and twigs, and then a thoughtful mood came over her.

That brown seed is dead now, thought she; but it will lie there in the dark a great while, and then green leaves will come up, and a stem will grow; and some day it will be a great tree. Then it will live. But, if it is dead now, how can it ever live? What a strange thing life is! What makes life? It can't be the sunshine; for that has fallen on these stones ever so many years, and they are dead yet: and it can't be the rain; for these broken sticks are wet very often, and they don't grow. What is life?

The child grew very solemn at her own thoughts, and a feeling as if some one were near troubled her. She thought the wind must be alive; for it moved, and very swiftly, too, and it had a great many voices. If she only could know now what they said, perhaps they would tell what life was. And then she looked up at the aged oaks, as they reared their arms to the sky, and she longed to ask them the question, but dared not. A small spring leaped down from a a rock above her, and fled past with ceaseless murmurs, and she felt sure that it lived, too, for it moved and had a voice. And a strong feeling stirred the young soul, a sudden desire to know all things, to hold communion with all things.

Now the day was gone, and the child turned homewards; but she seemed to hear in sleep that night the whispered question, "What is life?" She was yet to know.

The seed had been blown away from a pine tree, and it took root downward and shot green spears upward, until, when a few summers had passed, it had grown so famously that a sparrow built her nest there, among the foliage, and never had her roof been so water-proof before. There, one day, came a tall, fair girl, with quick step and beaming eyes, and sat down at its root. One hand caressed lovingly the young pine, and one clasped a folded paper. How she had grown since she put that brown seed into the earth! She opened the paper and read; a bright color came to her cheeks, and her hand trembled—

"He loves me!" said she. "I cannot doubt it."

Then she read aloud—

"When you are mine, I shall carry you away from those old woods where you spend so much precious time dreaming vaguely of the future. I will teach you what life is. That its golden hours should not be wasted in idle visions, but made glorious by the exhaustless wealth of love. True life consists in loving and being loved."

She closed the letter and gazed around her. Was this the teaching she had received from those firm old oaks who had so long stood before the storms? She had learned to know some of their voices, and now they seemed to speak louder than ever, and their word was—"Endurance!"

The never-silent wind, that paused not, nor went back in its course, had taught her a lesson, also, in its onward flight, its ceaseless exertion to reach some far distant goal. And the lesson was—"Hope."

The ever-flowing spring, whose heart was never dried up either in summer or winter, had murmured to her of—"Faith."

She laid her head at the foot of the beloved pine and said, in her heart, "I will come back again when ten years are passed, and will here consider whose teachings were right."

It was a cold November day. A rude north wind raved among the leafless oaks that defied its power with their rugged, unclad arms. The heavy masses of clouds were mirrored darkly in the spring, and the pine, grown to lofty stature, rocked swiftly to and fro as the fierce wind struck it. Down the hill, over the stones, and through the tempest, there came a slight and bending form. It was the happy child who had planted the pine seed.

She threw herself on the dry leaves by the water's edge, and leaned wearily against the strong young evergreen. How sadly her eyes roved among the trees, and then tears commenced to fall quickly from them. She was very pale and mournful, and drew her rich mantle closely around her to shield her from the wind. It had been as her lover had said. She had gone out into the world, had tasted what men call pleasure, had put aside the simple lessons she had learned in her childhood, to follow *his* bidding, to live in the light of *his* love. Ten years had dissolved the dream. The young husband was in his grave; the child she had called after him was no more. Weary and heart-broken, she had hurried back to the home she had left, and the haunts she had cherished.

She embraced the young pine, tenderly, and exclaimed—

"Oh, that thy lot was mine! Thou wilt stand here, in a green youth, a century after I am laid low. No fears perplex thee, no sorrows eat away thy strength. Willingly would I become like thee."

At last she grew calm; and the old question which she had never found answered to her satisfaction—"What is life?"—sprang up into her mind. All the deeds of past days moved before her, and she felt that hers had not been a life worthy of an immortal soul. She heard again the voices of the trees, the wind, and the stream, and a measure of peace seemed granted to her. "Endurance—Hope—Faith," she murmured. She rose to go.

"Farewell, beloved pine," she said. "God knows whether I shall see thee again; but such is my desire. With his help, I will begin a new existence. Farewell, monitors who have comforted me. I go to learn 'what is life.'"

In a distant city, there dwelt, to extreme old age, a pious woman, a Lydia in her holiness, a Dorcas in her benevolence. Years seemed to have no power over her cheerful spirit, though her bodily strength grew less. Great riches had fallen to her lot; but in her dwelling luxury found no home. A hospital—a charity school—an orphan asylum—all attested her true appreciation of the value of riches. In her house, many a young girl found a home, whose head had else rested on a pillow of infamy. The reclaimed drunkard dispensed her daily bounty to the needy. The penitent thief was her treasurer. Prisons knew the sound of her footstep. Alms-houses blessed her coming. She had been a faithful steward of the Lord's gifts.

Eighty-and-eight years had dropped upon her head as lightly as withered leaves; but now the Father was ready to release his servant and child. Her numerous household was gathered around her bed to behold her last hour. On the borders of eternity, a gentle sleep fell upon her. She seemed to stand in a lofty wood, beside a towering pine. A spring bubbled near, and soft breezes swept the verdant boughs. She looked upon the tree, glorious in its strength, and smiled to think she could ever have desired to change her crown of immortality for its senseless existence. Then the old question—"What is life?"—resounded again in her ears, and she opened her eyes from sleep and spoke, in a clear voice, these last words—

"He that believeth in the Son hath everlasting life. This is the true life for which we endure the trials of the present. For this we labor and do good works. A man's life consisteth not in the abundance of the things he possesseth; for to be spiritually-minded is life. I have finished my course; my toil will be recompensed an hundredfold; and I go to Him whose loving kindness is better than life."

A POETICAL VERSION.

OF A PORTION OF THE SECOND CHAPTER OF JOEL.

BY LADD SPENCER.

In Zion blow the trumpet,

Let it sound through every land;

And let the wicked tremble,

For the Lord is nigh at hand.

Alas! a day of darkness—

A day of clouds and gloom—

Approaches fast, when all shall be

As silent as the tomb!

As the morn upon the mountains,

There comes a mighty train,

The like of which hath never been.

And ne'er shall be again.

A burning fire before them,

And behind a raging flame—

Alas, that beauty so should be

Enwrapt in sin and shame!

The earth doth quake before them,

The sun withdraws its light;

The heavens and earth are shrouded

In darkest, deepest night.

Then weep, ye evil doers,

Let tears of anguish flow;

Your evil deeds have brought you

A load of endless woe!

TAKING BOARDERS.

BY T.S. ARTHUR.

CHAPTER I.

A lady, past the prime of life, sat, thoughtful, as twilight fell duskily around her, in a room furnished with great elegance. That her thoughts were far from being pleasant, the sober, even sad expression of her countenance too clearly testified. She was dressed in deep mourning. A faint sigh parted her lips as she looked up, on hearing the door of the apartment in which she was sitting open. The person who entered, a tall and beautiful girl, also in mourning, came and sat down by her side, and leaned her head, with a pensive, troubled air, down upon her shoulder.

"We must decide upon something, Edith, and that with as little delay as possible," said the elder of the two ladies, soon after the younger one entered. This was said in a tone of great despondency.

"Upon what shall we decide, mother?" and the young lady raised her head from its reclining position, and looked earnestly into the eyes of her parent.

"We must decide to do something by which the family can be sustained. Your father's death has left us, unfortunately and unexpectedly, as you already know, with scarcely a thousand dollars beyond the furniture of this house, instead of an independence which we supposed him to possess. His death was sad and afflictive enough—more than it seemed I could bear. But to have this added!"

The voice of the speaker sank into a low moan, and was lost in a stifled sob.

"But what *can* we do, mother?" asked Edith, in an earnest tone, after pausing long enough for her mother to regain the control of her feelings.

"I have thought of but one thing that is at all respectable," replied the mother.

"What is that?"

"Taking boarders."

"Why, mother!" ejaculated Edith, evincing great surprise, "how can you think of such a thing?"

"Because driven to do so by the force of circumstances."

"Taking boarders! Keeping a boarding-house! Surely we have not come to this!"

An expression of distress blended with the look of astonishment in Edith's face.

"There is nothing disgraceful in keeping a boarding-house," returned the mother. "A great many very respectable ladies have been compelled to resort to it as a means of supporting their families."

"But, to think of it, mother! To think of *your* keeping a boarding-house! I cannot bear it."

"Is there anything else that can be done, Edith?"

"Don't ask *me* such a question."

"If, then, you cannot think for me, you must try and think with me, my child. Something will have to be done to create an income. In less than twelve months, every dollar I have will be expended; and then what are we to do? Now, Edith, is the time for us to look at the matter earnestly, and to determine the course we will take. There is no use to look away from it. A good house in a central situation, large enough for the purpose, can no doubt be obtained; and I think there will be no difficulty about our getting boarders enough to fill it. The income, or profit, from these will enable us still to live comfortably, and keep Edward and Ellen at school."

"It is hard," was the only remark Edith made to this.

"It is hard, my daughter; very hard! I have thought and thought about it until my whole mind has been thrown into confusion. But it will not do to think forever. There must be action. Can I see want stealing in upon my children, and sit and fold my hands supinely? No! And to you, Edith, my oldest child, I look for aid and for counsel. Stand up, bravely, by my side."

"And you are in earnest in all this?" said Edith, whose mind seemed hardly able to realize the truth of their position. From her earliest days, all the blessings that money could procure had been freely scattered around her feet. As she grew up, and advanced towards womanhood, she had moved in the most fashionable circles, and there acquired the habit of estimating people according to their wealth and social standing, rather than by qualities of mind. In her view, it appeared degrading in a woman to enter upon any kind of employment for money; and with the keeper of a boarding-house, particularly, she had always associated something low, vulgar, and ungenteel. At the thought of her mother's engaging in such an occupation, when the suggestion was made, her mind instantly revolted. It appeared to her as if disgrace would be the inevitable consequence.

"And you are in earnest in all this?" was an expression, mingling her clear conviction of the truth of what at first appeared so strange a proposition, and her astonishment that the necessities of their situation were such as to drive them to so humiliating a resource.

"Deeply in earnest," was the mother's reply. "We are left alone in the world. He who cared for us, and provided for us so liberally, has been taken away, and we have nowhere to look for aid but to the resources that are in ourselves. These, well applied, will give us, I feel strongly assured, all that we need. The thing to decide is, what we ought to do. If we choose aright, all will, doubtless, come out right. To choose aright is, therefore, of the first importance; and to do this, we must not suffer distorting suggestions nor the appeals of a false pride to influence our minds in the least. You are my oldest child, Edith; and, as such, I cannot but look upon you as, to some extent, jointly, with me, the guardian of your younger brothers and sisters. True, Miriam is of age, and Henry nearly so; but still you are the eldest—your mind is most matured, and in your judgment I have the most confidence. Try and forget, Edith, all but the fact that, unless we make an exertion, one home for all cannot be retained. Are you willing that we should be scattered like leaves in the autumn wind? No! you would consider that one of the greatest calamities that could befall us—an evil to prevent which we should use every effort in our power. Do you not see this clearly?"

"I do, mother," was replied by Edith in a more rational tone of voice than that in which she had yet spoken.

"To open a store of any kind would involve five times the exposure of a boarding-house; and, moreover, I know nothing of business."

"Keeping a store? Oh, no! we couldn't do that. Think of the dreadful exposure!"

"But in taking boarders we only increase our family, and all goes on as usual. To my mind, it is the most genteel thing that we can do. Our style of living will be the same. Our waiter and all our servants will be retained. In fact, to the eye there will be little change, and the world need never know how greatly reduced our circumstances have become."

This mode of argument tended to reconcile Edith to taking boarders. Something, she saw, had to be done. Opening a store was felt to be out of the question; and as to commencing a school, the thought was repulsed at the very first suggestion.

A few friends were consulted on the subject, and all agreed that the best thing for the widow to do was to take boarders. Each one could point to some lady who had commenced the business with far less ability to make boarders comfortable, and who had yet got along very well. It was conceded on all hands that it was a very genteel business, and that some of the first ladies had been compelled to resort to it, without being any the less respected. Almost every one to whom the matter was referred spoke in favor of the thing, and but a single individual suggested difficulty; but what he said was not permitted to have much weight. This individual was a brother of the widow, who had always been looked upon as rather eccentric. He was a bachelor, and without fortune, merely enjoying a moderate income as book-keeper in the office of an insurance company.

But more of him hereafter.

CHAPTER II.

Mrs. Darlington, the widow we have just introduced to the reader, had five children. Edith, the oldest daughter, was twenty-two years of age at the time of her father's death; and Henry, the oldest son, just twenty. Next to Henry was Miriam, eighteen years old. The ages of the two youngest children, Ellen and Edward, were ten and eight.

Mr. Darlington, while living, was a lawyer of distinguished ability, and his talents and reputation at the Philadelphia bar enabled him to accumulate a handsome fortune. Upon this he had lived for some years in a style of great elegance. About a year before his death, he had been induced to enter into some speculation that promised great results. But he found, when too late to retreat, that he had been greatly deceived. Heavy losses soon followed. In a struggle to recover himself, he became still further involved; and, ere the expiration of a twelve-month, saw everything falling from under him. The trouble brought on by this was the real cause of his death, which was sudden, and resulted from inflammation and congestion of the brain.

Henry Darlington, the oldest son, was a young man of promising talents. He remained at college until a few months before his father's death, when he returned home, and commenced the study of law, in which he felt ambitious to distinguish himself.

Edith, the oldest daughter, possessed a fine mind, which had been well educated. She had some false views of life, natural to her position; but, apart from this, was a girl of sound sense and great force of character. Thus far in life, she had not encountered circumstances of a nature calculated to develop what was in her. The time for that, however, was approaching. Miriam, her sifter, was a quiet, gentle, retiring, almost timid girl. She went into company with reluctance, and then always shrunk as far from observation as it was possible to get. But, like most quiet, retiring persons, there were deep places in her mind and heart. She thought and felt more than was supposed. All who knew Miriam, loved her. Of the younger children we need not here speak.

Mrs. Darlington knew comparatively nothing of the world beyond her own social circle. She was, perhaps, as little calculated for doing what she proposed to do as a woman could well be. She had no habits of economy, and had never, in her life, been called upon to make calculations of expense in household matters. There was a tendency to generosity rather than selfishness in her character; and she rarely thought evil of any one. But all that she was need not here be set forth, for it will appear as our narrative progresses.

Mr. Hiram Ellis, the brother of Mrs. Darlington, to whom brief allusion has been made, was not a great favorite in the family—although Mr. Darlington understood his good qualities, and very highly respected him—because he had not much that was prepossessing in his external appearance, and was thought to be a little eccentric. Moreover, he was not rich—merely holding the place of book-keeper in an insurance office, at a moderate salary. But, as he had never married, and had only himself to support, his income supplied amply all his wants, and left him a small annual surplus.

After the death of Mr. Darlington, he visited his sister much more frequently than before. Of the exact condition of her affairs, he was much better acquainted than she supposed. The anxiety which she felt, some months after her husband's death, when the result of the settlement of his estate became known, led her to be rather more communicative. After determining to open a boarding-house, she said to him, on the occasion of his visiting her one evening—

"As it is necessary for me to do something, Hiram, I have concluded to move to a better location, and take a few boarders."

"Don't do any such thing, Margaret," her brother made answer. "Taking boarders! It's the last thing of which a woman should think."

"Why do you say that, Hiram?" asked Mrs. Darlington, evincing no little surprise at this unexpected reply.

"Because I think that a woman who has a living to make can hardly try a more doubtful experiment. Not one in ten ever succeeds in doing anything."

"But why, Hiram? Why? I'm sure a great many ladies get a living in that way."

"What you will never do, Margaret, mark my words for it. It takes a woman of shrewdness, caution, and knowledge of the world, and one thoroughly versed in household economy, to get along in this pursuit. Even if you possessed all these prerequisites to success, you have just the family that ought not to come in contact with anybody and everybody that find their way into boarding-houses."

"I must do something, Hiram," said Mrs. Darlington, evincing impatience at the opposition of her brother.

"I perfectly agree with you in that, Margaret," replied Mr. Ellis. "The only doubt is as to your choice of occupation. You think that your best plan will be to take boarders; while I think you could not fail upon a worse expedient."

"Why do you think so?"

"Have I not just said?"

"What?"

"Why, that, in the first place, it takes a woman of great shrewdness, caution, and knowledge of the world, and one thoroughly versed in household economy, to succeed in the business."

"I'm not a fool, Hiram!" exclaimed Mrs. Darlington, losing her self-command.

"Perhaps you may alter your opinion on that head some time within the next twelve months," coolly returned Mr. Ellis, rising and beginning to button up his coat.

"Such language to me, at this time, is cruel!" said Mrs. Darlington, putting her handkerchief to her eyes.

"No," calmly replied her brother, "not cruel, but kind. I wish to save you from trouble."

"What else can I do?" asked the widow, removing the handkerchief from her face.

"Many things, I was going to say," returned Mr. Ellis. "But, in truth, the choice of employment is not very great. Still, something with a fairer promise than taking boarders may be found."

"If you can point me to some better way, brother," said Mrs. Darlington, "I shall feel greatly indebted to you."

"Almost anything is better. Suppose you and Edith were to open a school. Both of you are well—"

"Open a school!" exclaimed Mrs. Darlington, interrupting her brother, and exhibiting most profound astonishment. "*I* open a school! I didn't think *you* would take advantage of my grief and misfortune to offer me an insult."

Mr. Ellis buttoned the top button of his coat nervously, as his sister said this, and, partly turning himself towards the door, said—

"Teaching school is a far more useful, and, if you will, more respectable employment, than keeping a boarding-house. This you ought to see at a glance. As a teacher, you would be a minister of truth to the mind, and have it in your power to bend from evil and lead to good the young immortals committed to your care; while, as a boarding-house keeper, you would merely furnish food for the natural body—a use below what you are capable of rendering to society."

But Mrs. Darlington was in no state of mind to feel the force of such an argument. From the thought of a school she shrunk as from something degrading, and turned from it with displeasure.

"Don't mention such a thing to me," said she fretfully, "I will not listen to the proposition."

"Oh, well, Margaret, as you please," replied her brother, now moving towards the door. "When you ask my advice, I will give it according to my best judgment, and with a sincere desire for your good. If, however, it conflicts with your views, reject it; but, in simple justice to me, do so in a better spirit than you manifest on the present occasion. Good evening!"

Mrs. Darlington was too much disturbed in mind to make a reply, and Mr. Hiram Ellis left the room without any attempt on the part of his sister to detain him. On both sides, there had been the indulgence of rather more impatience and intolerance than was commendable.

CHAPTER III.

In due time, Mrs. Darlington removed to a house in Arch Street, the annual rent of which was six hundred dollars, and there began her experiment. The expense of a removal, and the cost of the additional chamber furniture required, exhausted about two hundred dollars of the widow's slender stock of money, and caused her to feel a little troubled when she noted the diminution.

She began her new business with two boarders, a gentleman and his wife by the name of Grimes, who had entered her house on the recommendation of a friend. They were to pay her the sum of eight dollars a week. A young man named Barling, clerk in a wholesale Market Street house, came next; and he introduced, soon after, a friend of his, a clerk in the same store, named Mason. They were room-mates, and paid three dollars and a half each. Three or four weeks elapsed before any further additions were made; then an advertisement brought several applications. One was from a gentleman who wanted two rooms for himself and wife, a nurse and four children. He wanted the second story front and back chambers, furnished, and was not willing to pay over sixteen dollars, although his oldest child was twelve and his youngest four years of age—seven good eaters and two of the best rooms in the house for sixteen dollars!

Mrs. Darlington demurred. The man said—

"Very well, ma'am," in a tone of indifference. "I can find plenty of accommodations quite as good as yours for the price I offer. It's all I pay now."

Poor Mrs. Darlington sighed. She had but fifteen dollars yet in the house—that is, boarders who paid this amount weekly—and the rent alone amounted to twelve dollars. Sixteen dollars, she argued with herself, as she sat with her eyes upon the floor, would make a great difference in her income; would, in fact, meet all the expenses of the house. Two good rooms would still remain, and all that she received for these would be so much clear profit. Such was the hurried conclusion of Mrs. Darlington's mind.

"I suppose I will have to take you," said she, lifting her eyes to the man's hard features. "But those rooms ought to bring me twenty-four dollars."

"Sixteen is the utmost I will pay," replied the man. "In fact, I did think of offering only fourteen dollars. But the rooms are fine, and I like them. Sixteen is a liberal price. Your terms are considerably above the ordinary range."

The widow sighed again.

If the man heard this sound, it did not touch a single chord of feeling.

"Then it is understood that I am to have your rooms at sixteen dollars?" said he.

"Yes, sir. I will take you for that."

"Very well. My name is Scragg. We will be ready to come in on Monday next. You can have all prepared for us?"

"Yes, sir."

Scarcely had Mr. Scragg departed, when a gentleman called to know if Mrs. Darlington had a vacant front room in the second story.

"I had this morning; but it is taken," replied the widow.

"Ah! I'm sorry for that."

"Will not a third story front room suit you?"

"No. My wife is not in very good health, and wishes a second story room. We pay twelve dollars a week, and would even give more, if necessary, to obtain just the accommodations we like. The situation of your house pleases me. I'm sorry that I happen to be too late."

"Will you look at the room?" said Mrs. Darlington, into whose mind came the desire to break the bad bargain she had just made.

"If you please," returned the man.

And both went up to the large and beautifully furnished chambers.

"Just the thing!" said the man, as he looked around, much pleased with the appearance of everything. "But I understood you to say that it was taken."

"Why, yes," replied Mrs. Darlington, "I did partly engage it this morning; but, no doubt, I can arrange with the family to take the two rooms above, which will suit them just as well."

"If you can"—

"There'll be no difficulty, I presume. You'll pay twelve dollars a week?"

"Yes."

"Only yourself and lady?"

"That's all."

"Very well, sir; you can have the room."

"It's a bargain, then. My name is Ring. Our week is up to-day where we are; and, if it is agreeable, we will become your guests to-morrow."

"Perfectly agreeable, Mr. Ring."

The gentleman bowed politely and retired.

Now Mrs. Darlington did not feel very comfortable when she reflected on what she had done. The rooms in the second story were positively engaged to Mr. Scragg, and now one of them was as positively engaged to Mr. Ring. The face of Mr. Scragg she remembered very well. It was a hard, sinister face, just such a one as we rarely forget because of the disagreeable impression it makes. As it came up distinctly before the eyes of her mind, she was oppressed with a sense of coming trouble. Nor did she feel altogether satisfied with what she had done—satisfied in her own conscience.

On the next morning, Mr. and Mrs. Ring came and took possession of the room previously engaged to Mr. Scragg. They were pleasant people, and made a good first impression.

As day after day glided past, Mrs. Darlington felt more and more uneasy about Mr. Scragg, with whom, she had a decided presentiment, there would be trouble. Had she known where to find him, she would have sent him a note, saying that she had changed her mind about the rooms, and could not let him have them. But she was ignorant of his address; and the only thing left for her was to wait until he came on Monday, and then get over the difficulty in the best way possible. She and Edith had talked over the matter frequently, and had come to the determination to offer Mr. Scragg the two chambers in the third story for fourteen dollars.

On Monday morning, Mrs. Darlington was nervous. This was the day on which Mr. Scragg and family were to arrive, and she felt that there would be trouble.

Mr. Ring, and the other gentlemen boarders, left soon after breakfast. About ten o'clock, the door-bell rang. Mrs. Darlington was in her room at the time changing her dress. Thinking that this might be the announcement of Mr. Scragg's arrival, she hurried through her dressing in order to get down to the parlor as quickly as possible to meet him and the difficulty that was to be encountered; but before she was in a condition to be seen, she heard a man's voice on the stairs saying—

"Walk up, my dear. The rooms on the second floor are ours."

Then came the noise of many feet in the passage, and the din of children's voices. Mr. Scragg and his family had arrived.

Mrs. Ring was sitting with the morning paper in her hand, when her door was flung widely open, and a strange man stepped boldly in, saying, as he did so, to the lady who followed him—

"This is one of the chambers."

Mrs. Ring arose, bowed, and looked at the intruders with surprise and embarrassment. Just then, four rude children bounded into the room, spreading themselves around it, and making themselves perfectly at home.

"There is some mistake, I presume," said Mrs. Scragg, on perceiving a lady in the room, whose manner said plainly enough that they were out of their place.

"Oh no! no mistake at all," replied Scragg. "These are the two rooms I engaged."

Just then Mrs. Darlington entered, in manifest excitement.

"Walk down into the parlor, if you please," said she.

"These are our rooms," said Scragg, showing no inclination to vacate the premises.

"Be kind enough to walk down into the parlor," repeated Mrs. Darlington, whose sense of propriety was outraged by the man's conduct, and who felt a corresponding degree of indignation.

With some show of reluctance, this invitation was acceded to, and Mr. Scragg went muttering down stairs, followed by his brood. The moment he left the chamber, the door was shut and locked by Mrs. Ring, who was a good deal frightened by so unexpected an intrusion.

"What am I to understand by this, madam?" said Mr. Scragg, fiercely, as soon as they had all reached the parlor, planting his hands upon his hips as he spoke, drawing himself up, and looking at Mrs. Darlington with a lowering countenance.

"Take a seat, madam," said Mrs. Darlington, addressing the man's wife in a tone of forced composure. She was struggling for self-possession.

The lady sat down.

"Will you be good enough to explain the meaning of all this, madam?" repeated Mr. Scragg.

"The meaning is simply," replied Mrs. Darlington, "that I have let the front room in the second story to a gentleman and his wife for twelve dollars a-week."

"The deuce you have!" said Mr. Scragg, with a particular exhibition of gentlemanly indignation. "And pray, madam, didn't you let both the rooms in the second story to me for sixteen dollars?"

"I did; but"—

"Oh, very well. That's all I wish to know about it. The rooms were rented to me, and from that day became mine. Please to inform the lady and her husband that I am here with my family, and desire them to vacate the chambers as quickly as possible. I'm a man that knows his rights, and, knowing, always maintains them."

"You cannot have the rooms, sir. That is out of the question," said Mrs. Darlington, looking both distressed and indignant.

"And I tell you that I will have them!" replied Scragg, angrily.

"Peter! Peter! Don't act so," now interposed Mrs. Scragg. "There's no use in it."

"Ain't there, indeed! We'll see. Madam"—he addressed Mrs. Darlington—"will you be kind enough to inform the lady and gentleman who now occupy one of our rooms"—

"Mr. Scragg!" said Mrs. Darlington, in whose fainting heart his outrageous conduct had awakened something of the right spirit—

"Mr. Scragg, I wish you to understand, once for all, that the front room is taken and now occupied, and that you cannot have it."

"Madam!"

"It's no use for you to waste words, sir! What I say I mean. I have other rooms in the house very nearly as good, and am willing to take you for something less in consideration of this disappointment. If that will meet your views, well; if not, let us have no more words on the subject."

There was a certain something in Mrs. Darlington's tone of voice that Scragg understood to mean a fixed purpose. Moreover, his mind caught at the idea of getting boarded for something less than sixteen dollars a-week.

"Where are the rooms?" he asked, gruffly.

"The third story chambers."

"Front?"

"Yes."

"I don't want to go to the third story."

"Very well. Then you can have the back chamber down stairs, and the front chamber above."

"What will be your charge?"

"Fourteen dollars."

"That will do, Peter," said Mrs. Scragg. "Two dollars a week is considerable abatement."

"It's something, of course. But I don't like this off and on kind of business. When I make an agreement, I'm up to the mark, and expect the same from everybody else. Will you let my wife see the rooms, madam?"

"Certainly," replied Mrs. Darlington, and moved towards the door. Mrs. Scragg followed, and so did all the juvenile Scraggs—the latter springing up the stairs with the agility of apes and the noise of a dozen rude schoolboys just freed from the terror of rod and ferule.

The rooms suited Mrs. Scragg very well—at least such was her report to her husband—and, after some further rudeness on the part of Mr. Scragg, and an effort to beat Mrs. Darlington down to twelve dollars a-week, were taken, and forthwith occupied.

CHAPTER IV.

Mrs. Darlington was a woman of refinement herself, and had been used to the society of refined persons. She was, naturally enough, shocked at the coarseness and brutality of Mr. Scragg, and, ere an hour went by, in despair at the unmannerly rudeness of the children, the oldest a stout, vulgar-looking boy, who went racing and rummaging about the house from the garret to the cellar. For a long time after her exciting interview with Mr. Scragg, she sat weeping and trembling in her own room, with Edith by her side, who sought earnestly to comfort and encourage her.

"Oh, Edith!" she sobbed, "to think that we should be humbled to this!"

"Necessity has forced us into our present unhappy position, mother," replied Edith. "Let us meet its difficulties with as brave hearts as possible."

"I shall never be able to treat that dreadful man with even common civility," said Mrs. Darlington.

"We have accepted him as our guest, mother, and it will be our duty to make all as pleasant and comfortable as possible. We will have to bear much, I see—much beyond what I had anticipated."

Mrs. Darlington sighed deeply as she replied—

"Yes, yes, Edith. Ah, the thought makes me miserable!"

"No more of that sweet drawing together in our own dear home circle," remarked Edith, sadly. "Henceforth we are to bear the constant presence and intrusion of strangers, with whom we have few or no sentiments in common. We open our house and take in the ignorant, the selfish, the vulgar, and feed them for a certain price! Does not the thought bring a feeling of painful humiliation? What can pay for all this? Ah me! The anticipation had in it not a glimpse of what we have found in our brief experience. Except Mr. and Mrs.

Ring, there isn't a lady nor gentleman in the house. That Mason is so rudely familiar that I cannot bear to come near him. He's making himself quite intimate with Henry already, and I don't like to see it."

"Nor do I," replied Mrs. Darlington. "Henry's been out with him twice to the theatre already."

"I'm afraid of his influence over Henry. He's not the kind of a companion he ought to choose," said Edith. "And then Mr. Barling is with Miriam in the parlor almost every evening. He asks her to sing, and she says she doesn't like to refuse."

The mother sighed deeply. While they were conversing, a servant came to their room to say that Mr. Ring was in the parlor, and wished to speak with Mrs. Darlington. It was late in the afternoon of the day on which the Scraggs had made their appearance.

With a presentiment of trouble, Mrs. Darlington went down to the parlor.

"Madam," said Mr. Ring, as soon as she entered, speaking in a firm voice, "I find that my wife has been grossly insulted by a fellow whose family you have taken into your house. Now they must leave here, or we will, and that forthwith."

"I regret extremely," replied Mrs. Darlington, "the unpleasant occurrence to which you allude; but I do not see how it is possible for me to turn these people out of the house."

"Very well, ma'am. Suit yourself about that. You can choose between us. Both can't remain."

"If I were to tell this Mr. Scragg to seek another boarding-house, he would insult me," said Mrs. Darlington.

"Strange that you would take such a fellow into your house!"

"My rooms were vacant, and I had to fill them."

"Better to have let them remain vacant. But this is neither here nor there. If this fellow remains, we go."

And go they did on the next day. Mrs. Darlington was afraid to approach Mr. Scragg on the subject. Had she done so, she would have received nothing but abuse.

Two weeks afterwards, the room vacated by Mr. and Mrs. Ring was taken by a tall, fine-looking man, who wore a pair of handsome whiskers and dressed elegantly. He gave his name as Burton, and agreed to pay eight dollars. Mrs. Darlington liked him very much. There was a certain style about him that evidenced good breeding and a knowledge of the world. What his business was he did not say. He was usually in the house as late as ten o'clock in the morning, and rarely came in before twelve at night.

Soon after Mr. Burton became a member of Mrs. Darlington's household, he began to show particular attentions to Miriam, who was in her nineteenth year, and was, as we have said, a gentle, timid, shrinking girl. Though she did not encourage, she would not reject the attentions of the polite and elegant stranger, who had so much that was agreeable to say that she insensibly acquired a kind of prepossession in his favor.

As now constituted, the family of Mrs. Darlington was not so pleasant and harmonious as could have been desired. Mr. Scragg had already succeeded in making himself so disagreeable to the other boarders that they were scarcely civil to him; and Mrs. Grimes, who was quite gracious with Mrs. Scragg at first, no longer spoke to her. They had fallen out about some trifle, quarreled, and then cut each other's acquaintance. When the breakfast, dinner, or tea bell rang, and the boarders assembled at the table, there was generally, at first, an embarrassing silence. Scragg looked like a bull-dog waiting for an occasion to bark; Mrs. Scragg sat with her lips closely compressed and her head partly turned away, so as to keep her eyes out of the line of vision with Mrs. Grimes's face; while Mrs. Grimes gave an occasional glance of contempt towards the lady with whom she had had a "tiff." Barling and Mason, observing all this, and enjoying it, were generally the first to break the reigning silence; and this was usually done by addressing some remark to Scragg, for no other reason, it seemed, than to hear his growling reply. Usually, they succeeded in drawing him into an argument, when they would goad him until he became angry; a species of irritation in which they never suffered themselves to indulge. As for Mr. Grimes, he was a man of few words. When spoken to, he would reply; but he never made conversation. The only man who really behaved like a gentleman was Mr. Burton; and the contrast seen in him naturally prepossessed the family in his favor.

The first three months' experience in taking boarders was enough to make the heart of Mrs. Darlington sick. All domestic comfort was gone. From early morning until late at night, she toiled harder than any servant in the house; and, with all, had a mind pressed down with care and anxiety. Three times during this period she had been obliged to change her cook, yet, for all, scarcely a day passed that she did not set badly-cooked food before her guests. Sometimes certain of the boarders complained, and it generally happened that rudeness accompanied the complaint. The sense of pain that attended this was always most acute, for it was accompanied by deep humiliation and a feeling of helplessness. Moreover, during these first three months, Mr. and Mrs. Grimes had left the house without paying their board for five weeks, thus throwing her into a loss of forty dollars.

At the beginning of this experiment, after completing the furniture of her house, Mrs. Darlington had about three hundred dollars. When the quarter's bill for rent was paid, she had only a hundred and fifty dollars left. Thus, instead of making anything by boarders, so far, she had sunk a hundred and fifty dollars. This fact disheartened her dreadfully. Then, the effect upon almost every member of her family had been bad. Harry was no longer the thoughtful, affectionate, innocent-minded young man of former days. Mason and Barling had introduced him into gay company, and, fascinated with a new and more exciting kind of life, he was fast forming associations and acquiring habits of a dangerous character. It was rare that he spent an evening at home; and, instead of being of any assistance to his mother, was constantly making demands on her for money. The pain all this occasioned Mrs. Darlington was of the most distressing character. Since the children of Mr. and Mrs. Scragg came into the house, Edward and Ellen, who had heretofore been under the constant care and instruction of their mother, left almost entirely to themselves, associated constantly with these children, and learned from them to be rude, vulgar, and, in some things, even vicious. And Miriam had become apparently so much interested in Mr. Burton, who was constantly attentive to her, that both Mrs. Darlington and Edith became anxious on her account. Burton was an entire stranger to them all, and there were many things about him that appeared strange, if not wrong.

So much for the experiment of taking boarders, after the lapse of a single quarter of a year.

(To be continued.)

DEATH OF A YOUNG LADY OF SIXTEEN.

BY MRS. L.G. ABELL.

Oh, I cannot, cannot think of her without a starting tear;

So late, in youthful loveliness, I felt her presence near:

Her healthful form of fairest mould, I seem to see her still,

And to hear her sweet and gentle voice, as the voice of summer rill.

Her eye of blue, like azure sky of clear pure light above,

With soft silk fringes on the lids, shading the deepest love,

Was a light that gleamed from out the heart, and its rainbow hues revealed—

A ray from its own full happiness, too full to be concealed.

At twilight's calm and silent hour, on the hushed lake's quiet breast,

I saw her gliding joyously, as glide the waves to rest—

And music, too, was on the air, soft as Eolian strain;

But I thought not then that Death was near, a victim soon to gain.

Oh, can it be that this is life!—a thing so frail as this!

Like a lovely flower that only smiles to give one thought of bliss—

That blooms in light and beauty a fleeting summer day,

Then closes up its sweetness, and passes thus away?

How still she lies! her ringlets droop, of pale and soft brown hair—

Parted upon her marble brow, they fall neglected there;

Her cold hands folded on her breast, her round arms by her side—

How sad all hearts that knew her well that she so soon has died!

How she is missed from out each spot where she so late has been;

Her silent chamber thrills the heart with keenest throbs of pain;

Her music, too, of voice and string seems ling'ring on the ear,

Only to fill the heart with woe that its sound ye cannot hear.

How long life looked to her; its far and distant day

Seemed like the rosy path she trod, and perfumed all the way;

No tear but those for others' woe had ever dimmed her eye,

For her youth was cloudless as the morn, and bright as noonday sky.

But ah! how soon the light is quenched that shone so sweetly here—

And oh! if love to God was hers, it glows in a brighter sphere!

That strange, mysterious spark of mind, shrined in the frailest clay,

Now flames amid the seraph band in a "house" that will not decay.

This world we know is full of tombs, covered with fairest flowers;

But yet how soon we all forget, and think them *rosy bowers*!

We build our hopes of pleasure here, select a fairy spot;

But Death soon proves to our pierced souls that he has not forgot!

Oh! wisely, wisely let us learn that this earth is not our home;

'Tis but the trial-place of life—a race that's swiftly run:—

Our precious hours are links of gold in that mysterious chain,

That fastens to our life above its *pleasure* or its *pain*.

Reclining on a Saviour's arm, we then walk safely here;

He whispers holiest words to us, and wipes the falling tear:

If Death appears, He takes away his cruel, poisonous sting—

Then for a home of perfect bliss He plumes the spirit's wing.

THE JUDGE; A DRAMA OF AMERICAN LIFE.

BY MRS. SARAH J. KANE.

PERSONS OF THE DRAMA.

JUDGE BOLTON.

HENRY BOLTON, *son of the Judge.*

DR. MARGRAVE, REV. PAUL GODFREY, *Classmates and friends of the Judge.*

PROF. OLNEY, *Teacher of a Classical School.*

FREDERICK BELCOUR, *son of Madame Belcour.*

CAPT. PAWLETT, *friend of Fred. Belcour.*

LANDON, *Counselor at Law.*

SHERIFF.

CLERK OF THE COURT.

CRIER OF THE COURT.

OFFICERS OF THE COURT.

TWELVE JURYMEN.

DENNIS O'BLARNEY, *servant of Dr. Margrave.*

MICHAEL MAGEE, *servant of the Judge.*

CITIZENS, MESSENGERS OF THE COURT, WATCHMEN, &c.

MADAME BELCOUR, *a widow, cousin of the Judge, and presiding in his household.*

BELINDA, *daughter of Madame Belcour.*

LUCY, *daughter of the Judge.*

MRS. OLNEY, *wife of Prof. Olney.*

ISABELLE, *reputed daughter of Prof. Olney.*

RUTH, *waiting-maid at Judge Bolton's.*

SCENE—partly in the city; partly at Rose Hill, near the city.

TIME OF ACTION, twenty-four hours, commencing at 10 o'clock, A.M., and ending at the same hour on the following day.

ACT I.

SCENE I.—*A Doctor's study. Books and instruments scattered around. Table in the centre, strewn with books and pamphlets.* DR. MARGRAVE *seated by the table, cutting the leaves of a pamphlet.*

DR. MARGRAVE.

Thus, ever on and on must be our course:

Even as the ocean drinks a thousand streams,

And never cries "enough!"—the human mind

Would drain all sources of intelligence,

Yet ne'er is filled, and never satisfied.

And theory succeeds to theory

As regular as tides that ebb and flow.

This treatise will disprove the last I read.

Shade of Hippocrates! what creeds are formed,

What antics practiced with your "Healing Art!"

I will not sport with fate, nor tamper thus

With man's credulity and nature's strength.

No: I will gently coincide with nature,

And give her time and scope to work the cure—

Strengthening the patient's heart with trust in God,

And teaching him that genuine health depends

On true obedience to the natural laws

Ordained for man—not on the doctor's skill.

Enter DENNIS, *with a card to the Doctor.*

DENNIS.

The gentleman awaits you in the hall.

DR. MARGRAVE (*reading the card*).

"Reverend Paul Godfrey"—my old college chum!

Is't possible! (*To* DENNIS.) Bring him up, instantly.

[*Exit* DENNIS.

I have not seen him since our hands were clasped

In Harvard Hall:—I wonder if he'll know me.

(*Enter* REV. PAUL GODFREY.)

Ah! welcome! welcome!—You are Godfrey still.

The changes of—how many years have passed

Since last we parted?

GODFREY.

Thirty years;—and you—

MARGRAVE.

Are altered, you would say. I know it well.

My hair, that then was black as midnight cloud,

Is now as white as moonbeams on the snow.

The image that my mirror gives me back

I scarce believe my own—so pale and worn.

Would you have known me had we met by chance?

GODFREY.

Ay, ay—among a million—if you spoke.

There's the old touch of kindness in your voice;

And then your eye from its dark thatch looks out

Like beacon-light, soul-kindled, as of yore.

Warm hearts will hold their own, tho' frosts of age

May lay their blighting fingers on our hair.

MARGRAVE.

Thank Heaven 'tis so!—But you are little changed,

Save the maturing touch that manhood brings

When health and strength have won the victory,

And laid their trophies on the shrine of mind!

GODFREY.

My lot has been amid the wild, fresh scenes

Of Nature's wide domain; where all is free.

Life seems t' inhale the vigorous breath required

To struggle with the elements around,

And thus keeps Time at bay. Like good old Boone,

The patriarch hunter, in the forest wilds

I've found that God supplied, and healed, and blessed.

Men live too fast in cities.

MARGRAVE.

Not if they

Would give their energies a noble aim.

The opportunities to compass good,

And good effected—these are dates that give

The sum of human life.

GODFREY.

True; most true.

It is in cities where men congregate,

And good and evil strive for mastery,

The sternest strength of soul must needs be tested.

But all that stirs the passions makes us old.

'Twould wear me out—this round of ceaseless toil,

In the same range of artificial life;

And I must greet you with a traveler's haste,

And back to my free forest home again.

MARGRAVE.

'Tis well that every part and scene in life

Can find its actors ready for the stage,

And well that our wide land has scope for all.

And yet to feel that those who raised together

Their hope-swelled canvass when life's voyage began—

Like ships, storm-parted, on the world's rough sea—

Can sail no more in sweet companionship!

'Tis a sad thought! Of all our college friends,

But one, beside myself, is here to greet you.

GODFREY.

Who is he?—There is one would glad my heart.

When college scenes arise, yourself and Bolton—

MARGRAVE.

'Tis he I mean.

GODFREY.

What, Bolton? Harry Bolton?

I heard some fellow-travelers in the cars

Talking of one Judge Bolton, as the man

Who filled his orb of duty like the sun—

Shining on all, and drawing all t' obey.

Surely this cannot be our Harry Bolton—

The frank, warm-hearted, but most wayward youth.

Whose mind was like a comet—now all light.

Anon, away where reason could not follow.

He surely has not reached this grave estate

Of Judge!

MARGRAVE.

The same, the same—our Harry Bolton.

And better still, a man whom all men honor.

GODFREY.

I must see him. Let us go at once. I feel

A joy like that of Joseph's when he found

That his young brother Benjamin had come.

Though now the order is reversed, for here

The youngest claims the honors.

MARGRAVE.

No, not so.

Your order should be first in estimation,

And always is, where men are trained for heaven

And mine would be the second, were we wise,

And followed Nature as you follow God.

And Law is the third station on the mount,

When men are placed as lights above life's path

And Bolton is, in truth, a light and guide.

GODFREY.

Where shall I find him?

MARGRAVE.

In his place, to-day,

The seat of Justice. We'll go—it is not far

The cause is one of special interest:

I'll give its history as we pass along.

Wilt go?

GODFREY.

Ay, surely, surely. I am ready now.

It is the very place and time to see him.

[*Exeunt.*

SCENE II.—*A street. Crowds of people hurrying on.*

Enter PROFESSOR OLNEY and FREDERICK BELCOUR.

OLNEY.

You say the sentence will be passed to-day?

BELCOUR.

Most certainly; and crowds will press to hear it

Judge Bolton has a world-wide reputation,

And 'tis a cause to rouse his eloquence.

OLNEY.

I wish I could be there.

BELCOUR.

What should hinder?

'Twould but detain you for an hour or two.

OLNEY.

My pupils stand between. Yet Isabelle

Might hear the recitations; she does this

Often, when I am ill. A dear, good child:

She thinks her learning of no more account,

Save as the means to help me in my tasks,

Than though she only could her sampler sew

Yet she reads Latin like a master, and

In Greek bids fair to be a Lizzy Carter.

If she but knew I was detained—

BELCOUR.

A note

Would tell her this. Write one, and I will send it.

Here's paper, pencil—

[*Taking them from his pocket, OLNEY writes.*

OLNEY.

I shall trouble you.

BELCOUR.

No trouble in the least. Now, hurry on.

The court-room will be filled. I'll send the note—

[*Exit OLNEY.*

Or bear it, rather. She shall see me, too

Before she has the letter from my hand.

A proud, ungrateful girl:—reject my love!

[*Turns to go out.*

Enter CAPTAIN PAWLETT

PAWLETT

How, Belcour—what's the matter? You go wrong.

'Tis to the court-house all the world is going.

BELCOUR (*impetuously*).

Let the world go its way, and me go mine

We've parted company, the world and I.

When Fortune frowns, the wretch is left alone

PAWLETT.

Ah! true—I've heard of some embarrassments—

BELCOUR.

Embarrassments!—A puling, milliner phrase!
One of those tender terms we coin to throw
A sentimental interest round the bankrupt;—
As though he may recover if he choose.
Why, Pawlett, man, I'm ruined, if the plan
I've formed to-day should fail. It shall not fail.
I will succeed. And Isabelle once mine,
With cash to bear us to a foreign land,
I care not for the rest, though death and hell
Should stand at the goal to seize me.

[*Exit violently.*

PAWLETT (*looking after him*).

The fool!
He's in a furious mood—and let him rave—
He'll never win his way with Isabelle.
My chances there are better, but not good.
Young Bolton's in my way. He loves her well;
And she, I fear, loves him. But then his father

Is proud as Lucifer, and selfish too.

Ambition makes the generous nature selfish.

He'll ne'er consent his only son should wed

The portionless daughter of a pedagogue.

No, no. I'll tot these bitter waters out.

I'll give the judge an inkling of the matter.

I'll write a note—he'll think it comes from Belcour.

If I can drive young Bolton from the field,

Then Isabelle is mine.—I'll do it.

(*As* PAWLETT *is going out, Enter* DR. MARGRAVE *and* REV. PAUL GODFREY.)

GODFREY.

You say Judge Bolton lives in princely style.

Is he a married man?

MARGRAVE.

He has been married;—

Most happily married, too. His wife was one

Of those pure beings, gentle, wise, and firm.

That mould our sex to highest hopes and aims.

He loved her as the devotee his saint:

And from the day he wed he trod life's path

As one who came to conquer.

GODFREY.

I see it now.

The motive to excel was all he needed.

He had a vigorous mind, a generous heart,

An innate love of goodness and of truth.

But he was wayward, and he hated tasks.

Such men must have an aim beyond themselves,

Or oft they prove but dreamers. And with such,

Woman's companionship, dependence, love,

Are like the air to fire:—the smouldering flame

Of genius, once aroused, sweeps doubts away,

And brightens hope, till victory is won.

MARGRAVE.

'Twas thus with Bolton. To his keeping given

The weal of one so dear—then he bore on,

Gathering from disappointments fruitful strength,

As winter's snows prepare the earth for harvest.

And when his angel wife was taken from him,

She left him pledges of her love and trust,

A son of noble promise, and a daughter

To nestle, dove-like, in her father's heart,

And keep her place for ever. She is blind!

GODFREY.

I marvel not that Bolton has excelled,

And won a station of the highest trust,

If his warm heart enlisted in the work:

But the small cares, the constant calculations

Required to make, at least to keep, a fortune—

I never should have looked to him for these.

MARGRAVE.

'Twas luck that favored him; or Providence,

As you would say. A friend of his and ours.

De Vere, the young West Indian in our class—

You must remember him—he left to Bolton

All his estate. A hundred thousand pounds

'Twas said he would inherit.

GODFREY.

How happened this?

De Vere returned to Cuba, there to marry?

MARGRAVE.

He did, and had a family. But all

His children died save one, and then his wife.

And so he hither came to change the scene.

Bolton, just widowed then, received his friend

With more than brother's kindness, for their griefs
Bound them, like ties of soul, in sympathy.
De Vere was ill, and, with his motherless babe,
He found in Bolton's home the rest he sought.
And there he died, and left his little daughter
To his friend's guardian care; and to his will
A codicil annexed, unknown to Bolton,
That gave him all if Isabelle should die
Before she reached the age of twenty-one,
And die unmarried.

GODFREY.
She is dead, then?

MARGRAVE.
She is. Her life was like the early rose,
That bears th' frost in its heart. The bud is fair;
The strength to bloom is wanting; so it dies
But come, we shall be late.

GODFREY.
What crowds are going!
And Irishmen!—Are these so fond of Justice?

MARGRAVE.
Ay; where they feel she holds an even scale,

And is the friend alike of rich and poor,

They yield a prompt obedience, and become

Americans. Our motto is—"The law."

[*Exeunt.*

SCENE III.—*The Court-room. A crowd of people.* PRISONER *in the dock. His Wife, an infant in her arms, and his Sister, both in deep mourning, near him.* LANGDON, *counsel for the prisoner;* SHERIFF; CLERK *of the Court;* CRIER *of the Court;* CONSTABLES. *Enter* JUDGE BOLTON, *followed by two other* JUDGES. *All take their places on the bench. Then enter* DENNIS *and* MICHAEL.

DENNIS (*staring at the* JUDGE).

I' faith, 'tis a *purty* thing to be a judge,

And sit so high and cool above the crowd.

And your good master well becomes his seat.

He looks, for all the world, like Dan O'Connell.

MICHAEL.

He looks like a better man, and that's himself.

I wish he was judge of Ireland.

DENNIS.

So do I;

And my good *masther* was her doctor too.

They'd set the *ould* country on her legs right soon.

He's coming now.

Pointing to DR. MARGRAVE, *who is entering,*

followed by REV. PAUL GODFREY.

MICHAEL.

Who's with your master?

He looks as he had mettle in his arm.

DENNIS.

He is my master's friend—a sort o' priest.

MICHAEL.

And sure can battle with the fiend himself.

He looks as strong as Samson.

DENNIS.

Well for him

Living away in the West, 'mong savages,

And bears, and wolves, and—

CRIER OF THE COURT.

Silence!

MARGRAVE (*turning to* GODFREY, *who is gazing*

at JUDGE BOLTON).

You seem surprised. Has he outlived the likeness

Kept in your mind? Seems he another man?

GODFREY.

He is another man. The soul has wrought

Its work, as 'twere, with fire, and purified

The dross of selfish passion from his aims.

I read the victory on his open brow,

And in the deep repose of his calm eye.

MARGRAVE.

His was a noble nature from the first.

GODFREY.

He had a searching mind, a strong, warm heart,

And impulses of nobleness and truth.

But Nature sets her favorite sons a task:

We are not good by chance. Bolton had pride—

An overweening pride in his own powers.

This pride obeys the will; and when the brain

Is mean and narrow, like a low-roofed dungeon,

And only keeps one image there confined—

The image of self—the heart soon yields its truth,

And makes this self its idol, aim, and end.

Such is the Haman pride that mars the man,

And makes the wise contemn and hate him too—

Hate and contemn the more, the more he prospers.

MARGRAVE.

This is not Bolton's picture?

GODFREY.

No. His pride,

Now his strong lion will has curbed the jackals—

Those appetites and vanities of self

That mark the coxcomb rare wherever seen—

Is all made up of generous sentiments,

The father's, citizen's, and patriot's pride.

MARGRAVE.

You read him like a book.

GODFREY.

An art we learn

Of reading men when we have few books to read.

CRIER OF THE COURT.

Silence!

Enter two OFFICERS OF THE COURT, *attending the twelve* JURYMEN, *who take their seats. A crowd follows.* PROFESSOR OLNEY *trying to press through the crowd: young* HENRY BOLTON *makes room for him.*

YOUNG BOLTON.

Stand here, Professor Olney—take this place;

Here you will not be crowded. Ah! your cough

Is troublesome to-day. Pray, take this seat;

You'll see as well, and be much more at ease.

PROFESSOR OLNEY (*taking the seat*).

Thank you! thank you! This is kind, indeed.

I am not well to-day, but could not lose

This chance of listening to your father's voice.

His eloquence is classic in its style;

Not brilliant with explosive coruscations

Of heterogeneous thoughts at random caught,

And scattered like a shower of shooting stars

That end in darkness—no; Judge Bolton's mind

Is clear, and full, and stately, and serene.

His earnest and undazzled eye he keeps

Fixed on the sun of Truth, and breathes his speech

As easy as an eagle cleaves the air,

And never pauses till the height is won.

And all who listen follow where he leads.

YOUNG BOLTON.

I hope you will be gratified. Are all—

All well at home?

PROFESSOR OLNEY *(smiling)*.

I should not else be out.

And Isabelle will hear the recitations.

YOUNG BOLTON *(aside)*.

I'll go, and see, and help her. Not to conquer

As Cæsar boasted—she has conquered me.

I'll go and yield myself her captive.

[*Exit* YOUNG BOLTON.

CRIER OF THE COURT.

Silence!

CLERK OF THE COURT.

Gentlemen of the jury, are you ready

To give the verdict now?

FOREMAN.

We are ready.

CLERK OF THE COURT.

Prisoner, stand up and look upon the jury.

Jury, if and up and look upon the prisoner.

The man you now behold has had his trial

Before you for a crime. What is the verdict?

Is he, the prisoner, guilty or not guilty?

FOREMAN *(reading the verdict).*

Guilty of murder in the second degree.

[*A deep silence, broken only by the sobs of prisoner's wife and sister. Prisoner sinks down on his seat.* CLERK OF THE COURT *records the sentence.*

CLERK OF THE COURT.

Gentlemen of the jury, listen to

The verdict as recorded by the court

The prisoner at the bar is therein found

For crime committed—and that has been proven—

Guilty of murder in the second degree.

So say you, Mister Foreman? So say all?

FOREMAN AND JURY.

All (*bowing*).

JUDGE BOLTON.

A righteous verdict this, and yet a sad one

A fellow-being banished from our midst,

To pass his days in utter loneliness

Prisoner you've heard the verdict. Have you aught

To say why sentence should not now be passed?

Speak; you may have the opportunity.

LANGDON *counsel for the prisoner, confers*

with him then addresses the JUDGE.

LANGDON

He cannot speak; his heart o'erpowers his tongue;

The tide of grief seeps all his strength away,

As rising waters drown the sinking boat.

And he entreats that I would say for him,

The court permitting me, a few last words.

JUDGE BOLTON

Go on. You are permitted.

LANGDON.

May it please

The court, the jury, and all these good people,

The prisoner prays that I would beg for him,

As on his soul's behalf, your prayers and pardon:

That is, while he in penitence will yield

To the just punishment the law awards,

You'll think of him as one misled—not cruel.

The murderous deed his hand did was not done

With heart consent—he knew it not. The fiend

That *rum* evokes had entered him, and changed

His nature. So he prays you will never brand

His innocent boy with this his father's guilt;

Nor on his broken-hearted wife look cold,

As though his leprous sin defiled these poor

And helpless sufferers. Then he prays that all

Would lend their aid to root intemperance out,

And crush the horrid haunts of sin and ruin,

Where liquid poison for the soul is sold!

And while the victims of this deadly traffic

Must bear the penalty of crimes committed,

Even when the light of reason has been quenched,

That you would frame a law to reach the tempter,

Nor let those go unscathed who cause the crime.

And then he prays, most fervently, that all

Who may, like him, be tempted by the bowl,

Would lake a warning from his fearful fate,

And "touch not, taste not" make their solemn pledge,

And so he parts with all in charity.

[*A pause—the sobs of the prisoner's wife and sister are heard.*

CRIER OF THE COURT.

Silence!

CLERK OF THE COURT.

Prisoner, stand up and listen to the sentence.

JUDGE BOLTON (*solemnly*).

Laws hitherto are framed to punish crime

All legislators have been slow to deal

With vice in its first elements; and here

Lie the pernicious root and seeds of sin.

That children are permitted to grow up

From infancy to youth without instruction,

Is a grave wrong, and ne'er to be redeemed

By penal statutes and the prisoner's cell.

We leave the mind unfortified by Truth,

And wonder it should fill with wayward Error.

There's no blank ignorance, as many dream;

Each soul will have its growth and garnering.

As the uncultured prairie bears a harvest

Heavy and rank, yet worthless to the world,

So mind and heart uncultured run to waste;

The noblest natures serving but to show

A denser growth of passion's deadly fruit.

Another error of our social state—

We charter sin when chartering temptation.

We see the ensnarer, like a spider, sit

Weaving his web; and we permit the work.

How many souls Intemperance has destroyed,

Lured to his den by opportunities

The law allows! The prisoner at the bar

Is one of these unhappy instances.

The testimony offered here has shown

He bore a character unstained by crime.

Nay, more—an active, honest, prudent man,

Prisoner, you have appeared, since you came here

Five years ago. You came with us to share,

In this free land, the blessings we enjoy;

Blessings by law secured, by law sustained;

The impartial law that, like the glorious sun,

Sends from its central light a beam to all,

And binds in magnet interest all as one.

And you had married here, and were a father

And prospered in your plans, and all was well.

Nay, more—'tis proved you had a generous heart,

And had been kind to your poor countrymen,

The homeless emigrants who gather here,

Like men escaped from sore calamities,

Where only life is saved from out the wreck.

And one of these, an early friend, who died
Beneath the kindly shelter of your roof,
Left to your care his precious orphan child—
His only child, his motherless, his daughter.
And you received the gift, and vowed to be
A father to the little lonely one.
Where is that orphan now?—Must I go on?
'Tis not to harrow up your trembling soul.
I would not lay a feather on the weight
Stern memory brings to crash the guilty down.
But I would stir your feelings to their depths.
And bring, like conscience in your dying hour,
The sense of your great crime, that so you may
Repent, and Heaven will pardon. Here on earth,
Man has no power t' absolve such guilty deed.
Prisoner, one month ago, and you were safe—
A man among your neighbors well beloved,
And in your home the one preferred to all.
No monarch could have driven you from the throne
You held in th' loving hearts of wife and child.
Your coming was their festival; your step,
As eve drew on, was music to their ears.

The little girl, the adopted of your vow,

Was always at the door to claim the kiss

That you, with father's tenderness, bestowed.

Alas! for her—for you—the last return!

One fatal night you yielded to the tempter,

And drained the drunkard's cup till reason fled,

And then went reeling home, your brain on fire,

And, raging like a tiger in the toils,

You fancied every human form a foe.

And when that little girl, like playful fawn,

Unconscious of your state, came bounding forth

To clasp your knee and welcome "father home"—

You, with a madman's fury, struck her dead!

[*A shriek is heard from prisoner's wife.*

Prisoner, for this offence you have been tried,

And every scope allowed that law could grant

To mitigate the awful punishment.

No one believes that malice moved your mind;

But murdering maniacs may not live with men;

And therefore, prisoner, you are doomed for life

To solitary toil. Alone! alone! alone!

Love's music voice will never greet your ear;

Affection's eye will never meet your gaze;

Nor heart-warm hand of friend return your grasp;

But morn, and noon, and night, days, months, and years,

Will all be told in this one word—alone!

Prisoner, the world will leave you as the dead

Within your closing cell—your living tomb.

But One there is who pardons and protects,

And never leaves the penitent alone.

Oh, turn to Him, the Saviour! so your cell,

That opens when you die, may lead to heaven:—

And God have mercy on your penitence!

[*Prisoner sinks down, as the curtain slowly falls.*]

END OF ACT I.

SABBATH LYRICS.

BY W. GILMORE SIMMS.

GOD THE GUARDIAN.—PSALM XI.

How say ye to my soul,

As a mountain bird depart?

For the wicked bend the bow,

With the aim upon the heart.

In the Lord I put my trust—

The Great Giver of my breath—

He is mighty as he's just,

He wilt guard my soul from death.

On his holy throne he sits,

With his eye o'er all the earth;

But his shaft, that slays the vile,

Never harms the breast of worth.

The man of wrath he dooms

To the terror and the blight;

But his love the soul sustains

That walks humbly in his sight.

LET WELL ENOUGH ALONE.

BY MRS. EMMA BALL.

"A word spoken in due season, how good is it!" and how often is its influence more lasting and more beneficial than at the time of its utterance either speaker or hearer dreams of.

To illustrate. When about seventeen, I was, at my earnest solicitation, placed in a seminary, with the understanding that for one year I should devote myself to study, and thus become better fitted for future usefulness as a teacher. How I had wished for such an opportunity! How often had my wish been disappointed! and how narrowly I had escaped disappointment even then! But I was there at last, and everything seemed to be just as I would have it. Thus far I had studied unaided, and amid incessant interruptions. Now I could obtain assistance, and command the necessary leisure. The last four years I had passed in a crowded city. Now I breathed the purest atmosphere, and the scenery around me was of surpassing beauty. My window commanded the prettiest view; and, better still, I had no room-mate to disturb me with unwelcome chit-chat. Who could be happier than I? There was but one inconvenience, one drawback to the feeling of entire satisfaction with which, day after day, I looked around "my charming little room;" and that was the position of my bedstead. I did not like that; for the head was so near the door as to leave no room for my table; and consequently, as I could not place my lamp in perfect safety near my bed, I was compelled either to waste the precious hour before broad daylight, or to rise and study in a freezing room. "If I could only turn this bedstead round," thought I, "so that the head would be near the table, how many hours I might save!" and I resolved that, on the coming Saturday, I would make the desirable change. On the afternoon of that day, I was engaged to ride home with one of the teachers, and the morning I had intended to devote to sewing and study: "but no matter," thought I; "by a little extra effort I can accomplish all." Accordingly, when Saturday came I commenced operations; but, after removing the bed and mattress I discovered, to my great concern, that, although the bedstead would stand as I wished, yet I could not turn it thither without first taking it apart; and for this a bed-key was necessary. "Well," thought I, "it is worth the trouble;" so I procured a bed-key; and at length—at length—two of the screws yielded to my efforts. The others, however, *would not* yield. I tried and tried, but without avail; and, wearied and disappointed, I stood wondering what I should do. Just then, the door opened; and "Aunty," an old lady whose kindness and sound sense had already won my regard, stepped in. "What is the matter?" she exclaimed—"why, what has the child been about?" "I was trying to turn my bedstead so," said I, ruefully pointing towards the table; and I went on to explain why I had done so. "I dare say thou wouldst find it more convenient so," answered Aunty; "but it is quite beyond thy strength." "I see it is," sighed I. "I would have it turned for thee" she said; "but that is the most troublesome bedstead in the house: no one can do anything with it except John Lawton, and he won't be home till Monday." "What shall I do?" asked I. "I'll get Mary to come up and help thee fix it as it was before," answered Aunty. I drew a long breath. "Oh, never mind," said she, soothingly; "it is not quite so convenient this way, to be sure, but—" "I'm not thinking of the inconvenience now," interrupted I, "but of the time I've wasted. Why, I've spent nearly four hours over that foolish old bedstead. I was to have taken tea with Miss Mansell this afternoon, and I had expected to learn a good French lesson besides: but now the morning is gone, and a profitable time I've made of it!" "I should not wonder if it prove one of the most profitable mornings of thy life." rejoined the old lady, "and teach thee a lesson more valuable than thy French or thy music either." "What is that?" inquired I. "To let well enough alone." answered Aunty—and she smiled and nodded slowly as she spoke. "I'll let well enough alone after this, I promise you," said I. "People of thy ardent temperament seldom learn to do it in one lesson," replied she; "but the sooner thou dost learn it, the better it will be for thy happiness. However, I'll go now and send Mary to help thee." Mary came: but it was nearly two hours before my room resumed its usual neat appearance.

Some three months after, I learned that a young lady whom I had unwillingly offended, by declining to receive her as a room-mate, had spoken of me disparagingly, and greatly misrepresented various little incidents of our every-day intercourse. Surprised and indignant, I at once resolved to "have a talk with her;" but first I made known my disquietude to Aunt Rachel. "What shall I do?" asked I, in conclusion. "Not much," she answered. "Take no notice of it. I see she has been talking ill of thee; but she can do thee little or no real injury. Those who know thee won't believe her," "But those who don't know me—" interrupted I. "Won't trouble themselves much about it," she replied; "and if ever they become acquainted with thee, they'll only have the better means of judging thee truly." "If I say nothing about it, though," urged I, "she'll feel encouraged to talk on, and worse." "If thou dost find she is really doing thee an injury," returned Aunty, "I'll not dissuade thee from taking it in hand; but, as it now stands, it is not worth disturbing thyself about." "I could make her feel so ashamed," persisted I. "I don't doubt thee," replied she, laughing; "I don't doubt thee in the least: but in doing so, won't thou get excited? Won't thou sleep better, and study better, and waste less time, if thou just 'let well enough alone?'" "That seems a favorite maxim with you," observed I. "I have found it a very useful one," she answered; "and, had I known its value earlier in life, I might have escaped a good deal of suffering. Ten years ago, I had a kind husband, and a promising son, and slowly, yet surely, they were gathering a pretty competence. We thought we could gather faster by going south; but the location proved unhealthy, and in one season I lost them both by a bilious fever." Sympathy kept me silent. "You would not discourage all attempts to better one's condition?" I at length inquired. "By no means," answered Aunt Rachel; "for that were to check energy and retard improvement. I would only advise people—impulsive people especially—to think *before* they act: for it is always easier to avoid an evil than to remedy it. Thou art fond of History," she continued, "and that, both sacred and profane, abounds with examples of those who, in the day of adversity or retribution, have wished, oh how earnestly, that they had let well enough alone. Jacob, an exile from his father's house: Shimei, witnessing the return of David: Zenobia, high-spirited and accustomed to homage, gracing Aurelian's triumph, and living a captive in Rome: Christina, after she had relinquished the crown of Sweden; and, in our own days, Great Britain, involved in a long and losing war with her American colonies. Every-day life, too, is full of such examples." I asked her to mention some. "Thou canst see one," she answered, "in the speculator, whose anxiety for sudden wealth has reduced his family to indigence; and in the girl who leaves her plain country home, and sacrifices her health, and perhaps her virtue, in a city workshop. Disputatious people, passionate people, those who indulge in personalities, and those who meddle with what don't concern them, are very apt to wish they had let well enough alone. People who are forever changing their residence or their store, their clerks, or their domestics, frequently find reason for such a wish. Even in household affairs, my maxim saves me many an hour of unnecessary labor. Dost thou remember the bedstead?" she added, with a smile. "Yes, indeed," I answered; "I shall never forget that. The other day I was going to alter my pink dress into a wrapper, like Miss Mansell's; but the thought of that old bedstead stopped me; and I'm glad of it; for, now that I look again, I don't think it would pay me for the trouble." "Well, think again before thou dost notice Jane Ansley's talk," said Aunty. I followed her advice; and I have never regretted that I did so.

Dear old lady! I left her when that pleasant year was ended, and never saw her again. She has long since entered into her rest: but I often think of her maxim, and in many cases have proved its value.

I think of it when I see a man spending time and money, and enduring all the wretchedness of long suspense or excitement, in a lawsuit which he might have avoided; and which, whether lost or gained, will prove to him a source of continual self-reproach. When I see a business man who, by an overbearing demeanor and oppressive attempts to make too much of a good bargain, has converted a conscientious and peace-loving partner into an unyielding opponent: or, when I hear of a farmer who has provoked a well-disposed neighbor by killing his fowls and throwing them over the fence, instead of trying some neighborly way of preventing their depredations on his grain. When I have seen a teacher exciting the emulation of a jealous-minded child; or by threats, or even by ill-timed reasoning(?), converting a momentary pettishness into a fit of obstinacy—I have felt as if I wanted to whisper in her ear, "Do not seem to notice them; let well enough alone." When I see an envious mother depreciating and finding fault with a judicious and conscientious teacher till she has discouraged or provoked her, I think it likely that the day will come when both mother and children will wish that she had "let well enough alone." So, too, when I observe a mother forcing upon her daughters an accomplishment for which they have no taste: a father compelling his son to study law or physic, while the bent of his genius leads to machinery or farming: or a widow with a little property placing her children under the doubtful protection of a young stepfather. Vanitia is intelligent and well read, and appears to advantage in general society; but her love of admiration, her wish to be thought *superior*, is so inordinate, that she cannot bear to appear ignorant of any subject; hence she often tries to seem conversant with matters of which she knows nothing, and perceives not that she thereby sinks in the estimation of those whose homage she covets. Affectua is pretty and accomplished, and, two years ago, awakened goodwill in all who saw her. Latterly, however, she has exchanged her simple and natural manners for those which are plainly artificial and affected. What a pity these ladies cannot "let well enough alone!"

But I must stop, or my reader may exclaim: Enough—practice thy own precept—and let well enough alone.

SUSAN CLIFTON; OR, THE CITY AND THE COUNTRY.

BY PROFESSOR ALDEN.

CHAPTER I.

On a pleasant afternoon in August, two gentlemen were sitting in the shade of a large walnut tree which stood in front of an ancient, yet neat and comfortable farmhouse. Perhaps it would be more in accordance with modern usage to say that a gentleman and a man were sitting there; for the one was clothed in the finest broadcloth, the other in ordinary homespun. They had just returned from a walk over the farm, which had been the scene of their early amusements and labors.

"I don't know," said he of the broadcloth coat, "but that you made the better choice, after all. You have time to be happy; you have a quiet that I know nothing about—in truth, I should not know how to enjoy it if I had it."

"The lack of it, then," replied his brother, "can be no hardship. I have often regretted that I did not secure the advantages of a liberal education when they were within my reach."

"That is an unwise as well as a useless regret. If you had gone to college, you would, as a matter of course, have chosen one of the learned professions. Your talents and industry would, doubtless, have secured to you a good measure of success; but you would often have sighed for the peace and rest of the old farmhouse. Remember, too, that it and these lands would have passed into the hands of strangers."

"Perhaps you are right. Still, as I am now situated, I should be very glad to have the advantages and influence which a liberal education would bestow."

"I think you overrate those advantages. You are substantially a well educated man; and you can now command leisure to add to your information. If you should be in want of any books which it may not be convenient for you to purchase, it will give me great pleasure to procure them for you. I can do so without the slightest inconvenience."

"I am greatly obliged to you; and, if it should be necessary, I will, without hesitation, avail myself of your kind offer. I feel the deficiency of my education most sensibly in respect to my daughter. I find myself incompetent to take the direction of her opening mind."

"That is the very point I wish to speak upon. You must, my good brother allow me to take charge of her education. I owe it to you for keeping the old homestead in the family. It will give me great pleasure to afford her the very best advantages. Let me take her to the city with me on my return."

"We may, perhaps, differ in our estimate of advantages. I can conceive of none at present sufficiently great to compensate for the loss of her mother's society and example."

"No doubt these are very valuable; but girls must go away from home to complete their education, especially if they live in the country. Even in the city, a great many parents place their daughters in boarding-schools, and that, too, when the school is not half a mile distant from their residence."

"A great many parents, both in the city and country, do many things which I would not do."

"You are willing to do what is for the best interests of your child."

"Certainly."

"If you will allow Susan to go with me to New York, I will place her at the first school in the city. She shall have a home at my house; and my wife will, for the time being, supply the place of her mother."

"I fully appreciate your kind intentions; but I could almost as soon think of parting with the sunlight as with Susan."

"You forget the advantages she would enjoy. You are not wont to allow your feelings to interfere with the interests of those you love. I am sure you will not in this case. Think the matter over, and talk with your wife about it. She has an undoubted right to be consulted.

I must go and prepare some letters for the evening mail." So saying, he arose and went to his room.

The two brothers, Richard and Henry Clifton, had been separated for many years. When Richard was seventeen years of age, his father indulged him in his earnest desire to become a merchant. At a great pecuniary sacrifice, he was placed in the employment of an intelligent and prosperous merchant in New York; and when, at the age of twenty-one, he was admitted as a member of the firm, his patrimony was given him to be invested in the concern.

To his remaining son, Henry, Mr. Clifton offered a collegiate education. This offer was declined by Henry, not through lack of a desire for knowledge, but in consequence of a too humble estimate of his mental powers. When he became of age, a deed of the homestead was given him. Not long afterwards, his father was carried to his long home.

The business of the firm to which Richard Clifton belonged rendered it necessary for him to repair to a foreign city, where he resided for fifteen years. He was now on his first visit to his native place, subsequent to his return to the commercial emporium.

Susan, the only child of Henry and Mary Clifton, was just sixteen years of age. Her light form, transparent countenance, brilliant eye, and graceful movements, were not in keeping with the theory that rusticity must be the necessary result of living in a farmhouse, especially when the labors thereof are not performed by hireling hands.

From the first day of his visit, the heart of the merchant warmed towards the child of his only brother. Her delicate and affectionate attentions increased the interest he felt in her. That interest was not at all lessened by a distinct perception of the fact that she was fitted to adorn the magnificent parlors of his city residence. It was, therefore, his fixed purpose to take her with him on his return. Some objections, he doubted not, would be raised by his sober brother; but he placed his reliance for success upon the mother's influence. No mother, he was sure, could reject so brilliant an offer for her darling child.

The time spent by the merchant in writing letters, affecting operations in the four quarters of the globe, was passed by the farmer in thoughtful silence, though in the presence of his wife and daughter. He withdrew as he heard his brother coming from his room.

"Uncle," said Susan, "do you wish to have those letters taken to the post-office?"

"Yes, dear."

"Let me take them for you."

She received the letters from his willing hand, and left him alone with her mother.

"Your husband," said he to Mrs. Clifton, "has spoken to you of the proposition I made to him respecting my niece?"

"He has not," said Mrs. Clifton.

"I requested him to consult you. I proposed to take her home with me, and give her the very first advantages for education that the city can afford."

"You are very generous. But what did Henry say to it?"

"He does not like the idea of parting with her; but, as I understand it, he holds the matter under advisement till he has consulted you. I hope you will not hesitate to give your consent, and to use your influence with my brother, in case it should be necessary."

"I should be sorry to withhold my consent from anything which may be for the good of my child. So generous an offer should not be declined without due consideration. At the same time, I must frankly say that I do not think it at all probable that I can bring myself to consent to your proposal."

"What objection can be urged against it?"

"I doubt very much whether it will be for the best."

"Why not for the best? What can be better than a first rate education?"

"Nothing; certainly, taking that term in its true sense. A first rate education for a young lady is one adapted to prepare her for the sphere in which she is to act. If Susan were to go with you, she would doubtless learn many things of which she would otherwise be ignorant; but it may be a question whether she would be thereby fitted for the station she is to occupy in life. That, in all probability, will be a humble one."

"She has talents fitted to adorn any station, only let them receive suitable cultivation. She shall never be in a position which shall render useless the education I will give her. I have the means of keeping my promise."

"I doubt it not. But ought a mother to consent that one so young and inexperienced should be removed from home and its influences, and be exposed to the temptations of the great world in which you live? It is a very different one from that to which she has been accustomed."

"As to removing her from home, my house shall be her home, and my wife shall supply the place of her mother."

"I will give to your kind proposal the consideration which it deserves; but I must say, again, that it is very doubtful whether I can bring myself to consent to it."

"I can't say that I have any doubt about the matter," said her husband, who entered the room as she uttered the last remark. "To be plain, my dear brother, if there were no other reasons against the plan, I should not dare to place her in a family where the voice of prayer is not heard, especially as her character is now in process of formation."

Richard was silent. At first, he felt an emotion of anger; but he remembered that they were in the room in which their excellent father was accustomed to assemble his family each morning and evening for social worship. On no occasion was that worship neglected, even for a single day. After a long silence, he remarked, "You may think better of it, my brother," and retired to his room.

CHAPTER II.

For some time after Richard Clifton had exchanged the quiet of agriculture for the bustle of commercial life, he read his Bible daily, and retained the habit of secret prayer which had been so carefully taught him in childhood. But, at length, the Bible began to be neglected, and the altar of mammon was substituted for the altar of God. In his business transactions, the laws of integrity were never disregarded, nor was his respect and reverence for religion laid aside, but he had no time to be religious. When he became the head of a family, the Word of God lay unopened on his parlor table, and family worship was a thing unknown. Though God had guarded him at home and abroad, on the sea and on the land, and had made him rich even to the extent of his most sanguine expectations, yet he had forgotten the source of his prosperity, and had never bowed his knee in thanksgiving. The education of his wife, a daughter of one of the "merchant princes," had been such that she found nothing to surprise or shock her in the practical atheism of her husband's course.

On the morning after the occurrence of the events recorded in the chapter above, as Susan returned from the village post-office, she handed her uncle a letter. Having perused it, he remarked—

"I must return to the city tomorrow. Will you go with me, Susan?"

"I should be delighted to do so, if father and mother could go with me."

"I should be happy to have them go. But suppose they do not? You cannot expect to have them always with you."

"Must you go so soon?" said Henry. "You make a very short visit after so long a separation."

"I must return to the city to-morrow; but my presence will be needed there only for a day or two. If Susan will go with me, I will return here next week and spend a few days more with you."

The matter was referred to Susan for decision. Her desire to see the wonders of the great city, as well as to gratify her uncle, overcame the reluctance which she felt to be separated, even for so brief a period, from her happy home.

The preparations for her sudden journey required the assistance of several neighbors; and thus the news of her intended visit to the city spread quickly through the village. There was, of course, much speculation concerning it. Some said it was merely a passing visit. Others said she had been adopted by her wealthy uncle, and was thenceforth to be a member of his family. Some regarded the supposed adoption as fortunate, and rejoiced in it for Susan's sake. Others were envious, and were ingenious and eloquent in setting forth the evils which might ensue. Some were sorry to see one so young and innocent exposed to the temptations of a city life. A few were surprised that her parents should consent to have her leave them, even though it were to become the heiress of almost boundless wealth.

In the course of the evening, a number of Susan's friends called to bid her good-by. As each new visitor came, an observant eye might have seen that she was disappointed. Her manner indicated that she expected one who did not come. The evening wore away, the social prayer was offered, and they were about to separate for the night.

"Susan, dear," said her uncle, "I will thank you for a glass of water."

Susan took a pitcher and repaired to the spring, which gushed out of a bank a few yards from the house. She had filled her pitcher, when a well-known voice pronounced her name.

"Is it you, Horace?" said she. "I am away to-morrow."

"So I have heard. Are you going to live with your uncle?"

"Oh no. I am coming home in less than a week."

"I am sorry you are going."

"Are you?"

"I am afraid you will not want to come home."

"Why Horace!"

"Come back as soon as you can."

"I will."

"Good-by!" He extended his trembling hand, and received one still more trembling. It was carried to his lips. Another good-by was uttered, and he was gone.

It was well for Susan that her uncle was not sitting in his own brilliantly lighted parlor when, with blushing cheek and trembling hand, she handed him the glass of water. In the dim light of a single candle, her agitation passed unnoticed.

In the morning, after oil-repeated farewells, and amid tears not wholly divorced from smiles, Susan set out on her journey, and, on the following day, arrived at the busy mart where souls are exchanged for gold, and hearts are regarded as less valuable than stocks. She entered the mansion of her uncle, and was introduced to his polished and stately wife.

CHAPTER III.

No pains were spared by her uncle to amuse Susan and to gratify her curiosity. Mrs. Clifton, also, to her husband's great delight, put forth very unusual exertions tending to the same end. Still, Susan was far from being perfectly happy. She wanted a place like home to which she could retire when weary with sight-seeing and excitement. In her uncle's house, notwithstanding his manifest affection and the perfect politeness of his wife, she did not feel at ease—she felt as if she were in public. And then to sit down at the table and partake of God's bounties, when his blessing had not been asked upon them, and to retire for the night when his protection had not been invoked, detracted greatly from the enjoyment which her visit was in other respects adapted to afford. The week during which she was to remain had not elapsed ere she desired to return home. Of this desire she gave no voluntary indication, but exerted herself to appear (as she really was) thankful for the efforts designed to contribute to her happiness.

"What do you think of our niece?" said Mr. Clifton to his wife one morning, when Susan was not present.

"I think she will make a fine girl—that is, with due attention," said his wife. She would have expressed her meaning more accurately if she had said, "I think she will make a fine impression—will attract admiration, if her manners are only cultivated."

"Would you like to have her remain with us permanently?"

"I rather think I should. I like her very well." This was uttered in a very calm tone.

"What school would you send her to if she should remain?"

"I would not send her to any school. She is old enough to go into society; and all that she needs is a little attention to her manners."

"She is only sixteen years old."

"She is quite tall, and will pass for eighteen at least. If we make a school-girl of her, she can't go into society for a year or more to come."

"It was a part of my plan to give her a thorough education."

"It is a part of my plan to have some one to go into society with me."

"I do not believe her parents will consent to part with her, except on condition that she shall spend several years in one of our best schools."

"Then let them keep her and make a milkmaid of her. If I take a girl and fit her for society, and introduce her into the circle in which I move, I wish to be understood as conferring a favor, not as receiving one."

"My dear, you know that the ideas of those who have always lived in the country must, of necessity, be somewhat contracted. We must not judge them by the standard to which we are accustomed."

"We ought not to make the girl suffer for the follies of her parent, to be sure. You can say what you please to them about it, and then the matter can be left with her. She will be glad to escape the drudgery of school, I dare say."

"I think not. She has an ardent desire for knowledge; and the strongest inducement I can set before her to come to the city is the means it furnishes for gratifying that desire."

"There are other gratifications furnished by the city which she will soon learn to prize more highly. Let her once be at home here, and be introduced to society, and her desire for book-knowledge will not trouble her much. I know more about women than you do, perhaps."

Mr. Clifton was silent. The last remark of his wife made a deep impression upon his mind. Certain it was that his knowledge of woman was rather more extensive and of a different character from that which he had expected to acquire, when he lived amid the green fields of the country, ere the stain of worldliness was upon his soul.

"I like Susan," said Mrs. Clifton. "I think she will prove quite attractive. I have never seen a girl from the country who appeared so well. She has a quick sense of propriety, and will give me very little trouble to fit her for society."

"I am glad you like her," said. Mr. Clifton. "Her residence with us will make our home more cheerful; and, with your example before her, her manners will soon become those of a finished lady."

Mr. Clifton went to his counting-room, and his wife was left alone. The compliment her husband had just paid her inclined her to dwell with complacency upon the plan of adopting Susan. She liked her for her fair countenance and her faultless form, and her quick observation and ready adoption of conventional proprieties. Her presence, moreover, would attract visitors, who were now less numerous than when Mrs. Clifton was young. Her name, too, favored the idea of adoption. The difference between a real and an adopted child would not readily be known. She made up her mind to adopt her, and would have made known her determination to Susan at once, had not an engagement compelled her to go out.

CHAPTER IV.

While Susan was thus left alone for a little season, she employed herself in writing the following letter to her mother—

"My Dear Mother: I have been so long without any one to speak to (you know what I mean), that I must write you, though I hope to reach home almost as soon as this letter. I am treated in the kindest manner possible. My uncle, I think, really loves me, and I certainly love him very much. His wife is a splendid woman. She was once, I doubt not, very beautiful, and she looks exceedingly well now when she is dressed. She is very polite to me. I am, I believe, a welcome visitor; and she desires me to stay longer than I engaged to when I left home. I have not been out much, except with my uncle to see the curiosities with which the city abounds. I have seen but few of my aunt's friends. In truth, I suppose I have pleased her not a little by not wishing to be seen. I am from the country, you know; though she thinks I am making rapid progress in civilization. I judge so from the commendation she bestows upon my attempts to avoid singularity. I remember you used to commend me when I made successful efforts to govern my temper: aunt commends me for the manner in which I govern my limbs, or rather when they happen to move to please her without being governed. Last evening (I had not seen uncle since the day before at dinner), I was glad to find him in the parlor as I entered it. Aunt said to me, 'If you could enter the parlor in that way when company is present, you would make quite a sensation.' I can hardly help laughing to think what a matter of importance so simple a thing as putting one foot before the other becomes in the city. I suppose, if I were to live here, I should learn to sleep, and even to breathe, by rule. I was going to say to think by rule; but thinking is not in fashion. So far as I can learn, the thinking done here is confined to thinking of what others think about them. Aunt was originally taught to do everything by rule. Custom has become with her a second nature. Her manners are called fascinating; but to me they are formal and chilling. I suppose they are perfectly well suited to those who desire only the fascinating. You have taught me to desire something more.

"I find myself deficient in the easy command of language which seems so natural here. I have been astonished to find what an easy flow of polished and tolerably correct language is possessed by some with whom language might rather be regarded as the substitute for, than the instrument of, thought. It must be owing to practice; though it is a mystery, to me how persons can talk so smoothly, and even so beautifully, without ideas.

"I have seen a great many new things. I will tell you all about them when I get home. I long for that time to come, though it be only two days off. Every one has so much to do here, or rather in in such a hurry, that, were it not for my uncle's mercantile habit of keeping his word, I should not expect to see home at the appointed time.

"I am glad I came, for many reasons. I did not know so well before how little the external has to do with happiness. As persons pass by and look through the plate glass upon the silk damask curtains, they doubtless think the owner of that mansion must be very happy. Now I believe my dear father is far more happy than my uncle. I do not believe that my uncle's magnificent parlors (I use strong language; but I believe they are regarded as magnificent by those who are accustomed to frequent the most richly furnished houses) have ever been the scene of so much happiness as our own plain *keeping-room* has. I would not exchange our straight-backed chairs, which have been so long in the *home-service*, for the costly and luxurious ones before me, if the *adjuncts* were to be exchanged also. I long to sit down in the old room and read or converse with my parents, by the light of a single candle. I prefer that homely light to the cut-glass chandelier which illuminates the parlors here. I love to see beautiful things, and should have no objection to possessing them, provided the things necessary to happiness could be added to them. Of themselves, they are insufficient to meet the wants of the heart. Instead of being discontented with my plain home, I shall prize it the more highly in consequence of my visit to this great Babel. Do not think I am ungrateful to my dear uncle and to his wife for their efforts to amuse me and make me happy. I should not be your daughter if I were.

"Aunt has just come in, and has sent for me to her room. Kiss my dear father for me, and pray for me that I may be restored to you in safety.

"Your affectionate daughter,

"SUSAN."

(To be continued.)

SING ME THAT SONG AGAIN!

BY MISS E. BOGART.

Sing me that song again!

A voice unheard by thee repeats the strain;

And as its echoes on my fancy break,

Heart-strings and *harp-chords* wake.

Sing to my viewless lyre!

Each note holds mem'ries as the flint holds fire;

And while my heart-strings in sweet concert play,

Thought travels far away.

And back, on laden wings,

The music of my better life it brings;

For years of happiness, departed long,

Are shrined in that old song.

Its cadence on my ear

Falls as the night falls in the moonlight clear—

The darkness lost in Luna's glittering beams,

As I am lost in dreams.

Sing on, nor yet unbind

The chain that weaves itself about my mind—

A chain of images which seem to rise

To life before my eyes.

The veil which hangs around

The past is lifted by the breath of sound,

As strong winds lift the dying leaves, and show

The hidden things below.

I listen to thy voice,

Impelled beyond the power of will or choice,

And to those simple notes' mysterious chime,

My rushing thoughts keep time

The key of harmony

Has turned the rusted lock of memory,

And opened all its secret stores to light,

As by some wizard sprite.

But now the charm is past,

My heart-strings are too deeply wrung at last,

And harp-chords, stretched too far, refuse to play

Longer an answering lay.

The music-spell is o'er!

And that old song, oh, sing it nevermore

It is so old, 'tis time that it should die!

Forget it—so will I.

Let it in silence rest;

Guarded by thoughts which may not be expressed

There was a love which clung to it of old—

That love has long been cold.

Then sing it not again!

The voice that seemed to echo back the strain

Has filled succeeding years with discords strange

And won my heart to change

And thou mayst surely cull

Songs new and sweet, and still more beautiful:

Sing *new* ones, then, to which no memories cling—

Most memories have their sting.

COSTUMES OF ALL NATIONS.— SECOND SERIES.

THE TOILETTE IN ENGLAND.

CHAPTER I

Ancient authors disagree in the accounts they give of the dress of the first inhabitants of Britain. Some assert that, previously to the first descent of the Romans, the people wore no clothing at all: other writers, however (and, probably, with more truth), state that they clothed themselves with the skins of wild animals; and as their mode of life required activity and freedom of limb, loose skins over their bodies, fastened, probably, with a thorn, would give them the needful warmth, without in any degree restraining the liberty of action so necessary to the hardy mountaineer.

Probably the dress of the women of those days did not differ much from that of the men: but, after the second descent of the Romans, both sexes are supposed to have followed the Roman costume: indeed, Tacitus expressly asserts that they did adopt this change; though we may safely believe that thousands of the natives spurned the Roman fashion in attire, not from any dislike of its form or shape, but from the detestation they bore towards their conquerors.

The beautiful and intrepid Queen Boadicea is the first British female whose dress is recorded. Dio mentions that, when she led her army to the field of battle, she wore "a various-colored tunic, flowing in long loose folds, and over it a mantle, while her long hair floated over her neck and shoulders." This warlike queen, therefore, notwithstanding her abhorrence of the Romans, could not resist the graceful elegance of their costume, so different from the rude clumsiness of the dress of her wild subjects; and, though fighting valiantly against the invaders of her country, she succumbed to the laws which Fashion had issued!—a forcible example of the unlimited sway exercised by the flower-crowned goddess over the female mind.

With the Saxon invasion came war and desolation, and the elegancies of life were necessarily neglected. The invaders clothed themselves in a rude and fantastic manner. It is not unlikely that the Britons may have adopted some of their costume. From the Saxon females, we are told, came the invention of dividing, curling, and turning the hair over the back of the head. Ancient writers also add that their garments were long and flowing.

The Anglo-Saxon ladies seldom, if ever, went with their heads bare; sometimes the veil, or *head-rail*, was replaced by a golden head-band, or it was worn over the veil. Half circles of gold, necklaces, bracelets, ear-rings, and crosses, were the numerous ornaments worn at that period by the women. It is supposed that mufflers (a sort of bag with a thumb) were also sometimes used.

Great uncertainty exists respecting the true character of a garment much used by the Anglo-Saxon ladies, called a *kirtle*. Some writers suppose it to have meant the petticoat; others, that it was an under robe. But, though frequently mentioned by old authors, nothing can be correctly determined respecting it.

Little appears to be known concerning the costume in Britain under the Danes; but we are told that the latter "were effeminately gay in their dress, combed their hair once a day, bathed once a week, and often changed their attire."

The ladies' dress continued much the same till the reign of Henry the First, when the sleeves and veils were worn so immensely long, that they were tied up in bows and festoons, and *la grande mode* then appears to have been to have the skirts of the gowns also of so ridiculous a length, that they lay trailing upon the ground. Laced bodies were also sometimes seen, and tight sleeves with pendent cuffs, like those mentioned in the reign of Louis the Seventh of France. A second, or upper tunic, much shorter than the under robe, was also the fashion; and, perhaps, it may be considered as the *surcoat* generally worn by the Normans. The hair was often wrapped in silk or ribbon, and allowed to hang down the back; and mufflers were in common use. The dresses were very splendid, with embroidery and gold borders.

About the beginning of the thirteenth century, the ladies found their long narrow cuffs, hanging to the ground, very uncomfortable; they therefore adopted tight sleeves. Pelisses, trimmed with fur, and loose surcoats, were also worn, as well as *wimples*, an article of attire worn round the neck under the veil. Embroidered boots and shoes formed, also, part of their wardrobe.

The ladies' costume, during the reigns of Henry and Edward, was very splendid. The veils and wimples were richly embroidered, and worked in gold; the surcoat and mantle were worn of the richest materials; and the hair was turned up under a gold caul.

Towards the year 1300, the ladies' dress fell under the animadversion of the malevolent writers of that day. The robe is represented as having had tight sleeves and a train, over which was worn a surcoat and mantle, with cords and tassels. "The ladies," says a poet of the thirteenth century, "were like peacocks and magpies; for the pies bear feathers of various colors, which Nature gives them; so the ladies love strange habits, and a variety of ornaments. The pies have long tails, that trail in the mud; so the ladies make their tails a thousand times longer than those of peacocks and pies."

The pictures of the ladies of that time certainly present us with no very elegant specimens of their fashions. Their gowns or tunics are so immensely long, that the fair dames are obliged to hold them up, to enable them to move; whilst a sweeping train trails after them; and over the head and round the neck is a variety of, or substitute for, the wimple, which is termed a *gorget*. It enclosed the cheeks and chin, and fell upon the bosom, giving the wearer very much the appearance of suffering from sore-throat or toothache.

When this head-dress was not worn, a caul of net-work, called a *crespine*, often replaced it, and for many years it continued to be a favorite coiffure.

The writers of this time speak of tight lacing, and of ladies with small waists.

In the next reign, an apron is first met with, tied behind with a ribbon. The sleeves of the robe, and the petticoat, are trimmed with a border of embroidery; rich bracelets are also frequently seen; but, notwithstanding all the splendor of the costume, the gorget still envelops the neck.

SONNET.—WINTER.

BY LEWIS GRAHAM, M.D.

Stern Winter comes with frowns and frosty smiles,

The angry clouds in stormy squadrons fly,

While winds, in raging tones, to winds reply;

Old Boreas reigns, and like a wizard, piles,

Where'er he pleases, with his gusty breath,

The heaps of snow on mountain, hill, or heath,

In strangest shapes, with curious sport and wild;

But soon the sun will come with gentle rays,

To kiss him while with fiercest storms he plays,

And make him mild and quiet as a child.

Though now the bleak wind-king so boisterous seems,

And drives the tempest madly o'er the plain,

He smiles in Spring-time soft as April rain,

In Summer sleeps on flowers in zephyr-dreams.

BUBBLES.

BY JOHN NEAL.

"Hurrah for bubbles! I go for bubbles, my dear," stopping for a moment on his way through the large drawing-rooms, and looking at his wife and the baby very much as a painter might do while in labor with a new picture. "Bubbles are the only things worth living for."

"Bubbles, Peter!—be quiet, baby!—hush, my love, hush! Papa can't take you now."

Baby jumps at the table.

"Confound the imp! There goes the inkstand!"

"Yes, my dear; and the spectacles, and the lamp, and all your papers. And what, else could you expect, pray? Here he's been trying to make you stop and speak to him, every time you have gone by the table, for the last half hour, and holding out his little arms to you; while you have been walking to and fro as if you were walking for a wager, with your eyes rolled up in your head, muttering to yourself—mutter, mutter, mutter—and taking no more notice of him, poor little fellow, than if he was a rag-baby, or belonged to somebody else!"

"Oh, don't bother! *Little arms*, indeed!—about the size of my leg! I do wish he'd be quiet. I'm working out a problem."

"A problem! fiddle-de-dee—hush, baby! A magazine article, more like—*will* you hush?"

Papa turns away in despair, muttering, with a voice that grows louder and louder as he warms up—

"Wisdom and wit are bubbles! Atoms and systems into ruin, hurled! And now a *bubble* burst! And now a WORLD! I have it, hurrah! *Can't* you keep that child still?"

"Man alive, I wish you'd try yourself!"

"Humph! What the plague is he up for at this time o' night, hey?"

"At this time o' night! Why what on earth are you thinking of? It is only a little after five, my dear."

"Well, and what if it is? Ought to have been a-bed and asleep two hours ago."

"And so he was, my love; but you can't expect him to sleep *all* the time—there! there!"—trotting baby with all her might—"Hush-a-bye-baby on the tree top—there! there!—papa's gone a-huntin'—"

"My dear!"

"My love!"

"Look at me, will you? How on earth is a fellow to marshal his thoughts—will you be quiet, sir?—to marshal his thoughts 'the way they should go'—Mercy on us, he'll split his throat!"

"Or train up a child the way he should go, hey?"

"Thunder and lightning, he'll drive me distracted! I wonder if there is such a thing as a ditch or a horsepond anywhere in the neighborhood."

"Oh! that reminds me of something, my love. I ought to have mentioned it before. The cistern's out."

"The cistern's out, hey? Well, what if it is? Are we to have this kicking and squalling till the cistern's full again, hey?"

"Why what possesses you?"

"Couldn't see the connection, that's all. I ask for a horsepond or a ditch, and you tell me the cistern's out. If it were full, there might be some hope for me," looking savagely at the baby, "I suppose it's deep enough."

"For shame!—do hush, baby, will ye? Tuddy, tuddy, how he bawls!"

"Couldn't you tighten the cap-strings a little, my dear?"

"Monster! get away, will you?'

"Or cram your handkerchief down his throat, or your knitting-work, or the lamp-rug?"

"Ah, well thought of, my dear. Have you seen Mr. Smith?"

"What Smith?"

"George, I believe. The man you buy your oil of, and your groceries.—Hush, baby! He's been here two or three times after you this week."

"Hang Mr. Smith!"

"With all my heart, my love. But, if the quarter's rent is not paid, you know, and the grocer's bill, and the baker's, and the butcher's, and if you don't manage to get the bottling-house fixed up, and some other little matters attended to, I don't exactly see how the hanging of poor Mr. Smith would help us."

"Oh hush, will you?"

The young wife turned and kissed the baby, with her large indolent eyes fixed upon the door somewhat nervously. She had touched the bell more than once without being seen by her husband.

"Wisdom and wit," continued papa, with a voice like that of a man who has overslept himself and hopes to make up for lost time by walking very fast, and talking very little to the purpose—"Wisdom and wit are bubbles"—

The young wife nodded with a sort of a smile, and the baby, rolling over in her lap, let fly both heels? at the nurse, who had crept in slyly, as if intent to lug him off to bed without his knowledge. But he was not in a humor to be trifled with; and so he flopped over on the other side, and, tumbling head over heels upon the floor, very much at large, lay there kicking and screaming till he grew black in the face. But the girl persisted, nevertheless, in lifting him up and lugging him off to the door, notwithstanding his outcries and the expostulatory looks of both papa and mamma—her wages were evidently in arrears, a whole quarter, perhaps.

"Wisdom and wit are bubbles," continued papa; "dominion and power, and beauty and strength"—

"And gingerbread and cheese," added mamma, in reply to something said by the girl in a sort of stage-whisper.

Whereupon papa, stopping short, and looking at mamma for a few moments, puzzled and well nigh speechless, gasped out—

"And *gingerbread and cheese!* Why, what the plague do you mean, Sarah?"

"Nothing else for tea, my love, so Bridget says. Not a pound o' flour in the house; not so much as a loaf, nor a roll, nor a muffin to be had for love or money—so Bridget says."

"Nothin' to be had without *money*, ma'am; that's what I said."

"Bridget!"

"*Sir!*"

That "*sir!*"—it was an admission of two quarters in arrear at least.

"Take that child to bed this moment! Begone! I'll bear this no longer."

The girl stared, muttered, grabbed the baby, and flung away with such an air—three quarters due, if there was a single day!—banged the door to after her, and bundled off up the front stairs at a hand-gallop, her tread growing heavier, and her voice louder and louder with every plunge.

"*Sarah!*"

"*Peter!*"

"I wonder you can put up with such insolence. That girl is getting insufferable."

The poor wife looked up in amazement, but opened not her mouth; and the husband continued walking the floor with a tread that shook the whole house, and stopping occasionally, as if to watch the effect, or to see how much further he might go without injury to his own health.

"How often have I told you, my dear, that if a woman would be respected by her own servants, she must respect herself, and never allow a word nor a look of impertinence—*never! never!*—not even a look! Why, Sarah, life itself would be a burthen to me. Upon my word," growing more and more in earnest every moment—"Upon my word, I believe I should hang myself! And how *you* can bear it—you, with a nature so gentle and so affectionate, and so—I declare to you"—

"Pray don't speak so loud, my love. The people that are going by the window stop and look up towards the house. And what will the Peabodys think?"

"What do I care! Let them think what they please. Am I to regulate the affairs of my household by what a neighbor may happen to think, hey? The fact is, my dear Sarah—you must excuse me, I don't want to hurt your feelings—but, the fact is, you ought to have had the child put to bed three hours ago."

"*Three* hours ago!"

"Yes, *three* hours ago; and that would have prevented all this trouble."

Not a word from the young, patient wife; but she turned away hurriedly, and there was a twinkle, as of a rain-drop, falling through the lamplight.

A dead silence followed. After a few more turns, the husband stopped, and, with something of self-reproach in his tone, said—

"I take it for granted there is nothing the matter with the boy?"

No answer.

"Have you any idea what made him cry so terribly? Teething, perhaps."

No answer.

"Or the colic. You do not answer me, Sarah. It cannot be that you have allowed that girl to put him to bed, if there is anything the matter with him, poor little fellow!"

The young wife looked up, sorrowing and frightened.

"The measles are about, you know, and the scarlet fever, and the hooping-cough, and the mumps; but, surely, a mother who is with her child all night long and all day long ought to be able to see the symptoms of any and every ailment before they would be suspected by another. And if it should so happen"—

The poor wife could be silent no longer.

"The child is well enough," said she, somewhat stoutly. "He was never better in his life. But he wanted his papa to take him, and he wouldn't; and reaching after him he tipped over the lamp, and then—and then"—and here she jumped up to leave the room; but her husband was too quick for her.

"That child's temper will be ruined," said papa.

"To be sure it will," said mamma; "and I've always said so."

She couldn't help it; but she was very sorry, and not a little flurried when her husband, turning short upon her, said—

"I understand you, Sarah. Perhaps he wanted me to take him up to bed?"

No answer.

"I wonder if he expects me to do that for him till he is married? *Little arms*, indeed!"

No answer.

"Or till he is wanted to do as much for me?"

No answer; not even a smile.

And now the unhappy father, by no means ready to give up, though not at all satisfied with himself, begins walking the floor anew and muttering to himself, and looking sideways at his dear patient wife, who has gone back to the table, and is employed in getting up another large basket of baby-things, with trembling lips and eyes running over in bashful thankfulness and silence.

"Well, well, there is no help for it, I dare say. As we brew we must bake. It would be not merely unreasonable, but silly—foolish—absolutely foolish—whew!—to ask of a woman, however admirable her disposition may be, for a—for a straightforward—Why what the plague are you laughing at, Sarah? What have you got there?"

Without saying a word, mamma pushed over towards him a new French caricature, just out, representing a man well wrapped up in a great coat with large capes, and long boots, and carrying an umbrella over his own head, from which is pouring a puddle of water down the back of a delicate fashionable woman—his wife, anybody might know—wearing thin slippers and a very thin muslin dress, and making her way through the gutters on tip-toe, with the legend, "You are never satisfied!" "*Tu n'est jamais contente!*"

Instead of gulping down the joke, and laughing heartily—or making believe laugh, which is the next best thing, in all such cases—papa stood upon his dignity, and, after an awful pause, went on talking to himself pretty much as follows:—

"According to Shakspeare—and what higher authority can we have?—reputation itself is but a *bubble*, blown by the cannon's mouth: and therefore do I say, and stick to it—hurrah for bubbles!"

The young wife smiled; but her eyes were fixed upon a very small cap, with a mournful and touching expression, and her delicate fingers were busy upon its border with that regular, steady, incessant motion which, beginning soon after marriage, ends only with sickness or death.

"*And*," continued papa—"*and*, if Moore is to be believed, the great world itself, with all its wonders and its glories—the past, the present, and the future, is but a '*fleeting show*.'"

The young wife nodded, and fell to dancing the baby's cap on the tips of her fingers.

"And what are *bubbles*," continued papa, "what are *bubbles* but a 'fleeting show?'"

The little cap canted over o' one side, and there was a sort of a giggle, just the least bit in the world, it was *so* cunning, as papa added, in unspeakable solemnity—

"And so, too, everything we covet, everything we love, and everything we revere on earth, are but emptiness and vanity."

Here a nod from the little cap, mounted on the mother's fingers, brought papa to a full stop—a change of look followed—a downright smile—and then a much pleasanter sort of speech—and then, as you live, a kiss!

"And what are *bubbles*, I should be glad to know, but emptiness and vanity?" continues papa.

"By all this, I am to understand that a wife is a bubble—hey?"

"To be sure."

"And the baby?"

"Another."

"And what are husbands?"

"Bubbles of a large growth."

"Agreed!—I have nothing more to say."

"Look about you. Watch the busiest man you know—the wisest, the greatest, among the renowned, the ambitious, and the mighty of earth, and tell me if you can see one who does not spend his life blowing bubbles in the sunshine—through the stump of a tobacco pipe. What living creature did you ever know—"

"Did you speak to me, my dear?"

"No. Sarah, I was speaking to posterity."

Another nod from the little cap, and papa grows human.

"Yes!—what living creature did you ever know who was not more of a bubble-hunter than he was anything else? We are all schemers—even the wisest and the best—all visionaries, my dear."

By this time, papa had got mamma upon his knee, and the rest of the conversation was at least an octave lower.

"Even so, my love. And what, after all, is the looming at sea; the Fata Morgana in the Straits of Messina, near Reggio; or the Mirage of the Desert, in Egypt and Persia, but a sample of those glittering phantasmagoria, which are called *chateaux en Espagne*, or castles in the air, by the wondrous men who spend their lives in piling them up, story upon story, turrets, towers, and steeples—domes, and roofs, and pinnacles? and *therefore* do I say again, hurrah for bubbles!"

"What say you to the South Sea bubble, my dear?"

"What say I!—just what I say of the Tulip bubble, of the Mississippi Scheme, of the Merino Sheep enterprise, of the Down-East Timber lands, of the Morus Multicaulis, of the California fever, and the Cuba hallucination. They are periodical outbreaks of commercial enterprise, unavoidable in the very nature of things, and never long, nor safely postponed; growing out of a plethora—never out of a scarcity—a plethora of wealth and population, and corresponding, in the regularity of their returns, with the plague and the cholera."

"And these are what you have called *bubbles*?"

"Precisely."

"And yet, if I understood you aright, when you said, 'I go for bubbles—hurrah for bubbles'—you meant to speak well of them?"

"To be sure I did—certainly—yes—no—so far as a magazine article goes, I did."

"But a magazine article, my love—bear with me, I pray you—ought to be something better than a brilliant paradox, hey?"

"Go on—I like this."

"If you will promise not to be angry."

"I do."

"Well, then—however *telling* it may be to hurrah for bubbles, and to call your wife a bubble, and your child another; because the world is all a 'fleeting show,' and bubbles are a 'fleeting show;' or because the Scriptures tell us that everything here is emptiness and vanity—and bubbles are emptiness and vanity; I have the whole of your argument, I believe?—is hardly worthy of a man, who, in writing, would wish to make his fellow-man better or wiser—"

"Well done the bubble!—I never heard *you* reason before: keep it up, my dear."

"You never gave me a chance; and, by the way, there is one bubble you have entirely overlooked."

"And what is that—marriage?"

"No."

"The buried treasures, and the cross of pure gold, a foot and a half long, you were talking with that worthy man about, last winter, when I came upon you by surprise, and found you both sitting together in the dark—and whispering *so* mysteriously?"

"Captain Watts, you mean, the lighthouse keeper?"

"Yes. Upon my word, Peter, I began to think you were *up* for California. I never knew you so absent in all your life as you were, day after day, for a long while after that conversation."

"The very thing, my dear!—and as I happen to know most of the parties, and was in communication for three whole years with the leader of the enterprise, I do think it would be one of the very best illustrations to be found, in our day, of that strange, steadfast, unquenchable faith, which upholds the bubble-hunter through all the sorrows and all the discouragements of life, happen what may: and you shall have the credit of suggesting that story. But then, look you, my dear—if I content myself with telling the simple truth, nobody will believe me."

"Try it."

"I will!—Good night, my dear."

"Don't make a long story of it, I beseech you.—Good night!"

"Hadn't you better leave the little cap with me? It may keep you awake, my dear."

"Nonsense. Good night!" and papa drops into a chair, makes a pen, and goes to work as follows:—

Now for it: here goes! In the year 1841, there was a man living at Portland, Maine, whose life, were it faithfully written out, would be one of the most amusing, perhaps one of the most instructive, books of our day. Energetic, hopeful, credulous to a proverb, and yet sagacious enough to astonish everybody when he prospered, and to set everybody laughing at him when he did not, he had gone into all sorts of speculation, head over heels, in the course of a few years, and failed in everything he undertook. At one time, he was a retail dry-goods dealer, and failed: then a manufacturer by water power of cheap household furniture, and failed again: then a large hay-dealer: then a holder of nobody knows how many shares in the Marr Estate, whereby he managed to feather his nest very handsomely, they say; then he went into the land business, and bought and sold township after township, till he was believed to be worth half a million, and used to give away a tithe of his profits to poor widows, at the rate of ten thousand dollars a year; offering the cash, but always giving on interest—simple interest—which was never paid—failed: tried his hand at working Jewell's Island, in Casco Bay, at one time, for copperas; and at another, for treasures buried there by Captain Kyd. Let us call him Colonel Jones, for our present purpose; that being a name he went by, at a pinch, for a short period.

Well, one day he called upon me—it was in the year 1842, I should say—and, shutting the door softly, and looking about, as if to make sure that no listeners were nigh, and speaking in a low voice, he asked if I had a few minutes to spare.

I bowed.

He then drew his chair up close to mine, so near as to touch, and, looking me straight in the eyes, asked if I was a believer in animal magnetism; waiting, open-mouthed, for my answer.

"Certainly," said I.

Whereupon he drew a long breath, and fell to rubbing his hands with great cheerfulness and pertinacity.

"In clairvoyance, too—*perhaps*?"

"Most assuredly—up to a certain point."

"I knew it! I knew it!" jumping up and preparing to go. "Just what I wanted—that's enough—I'm satisfied—good-by!"

"Stop a moment, my good fellow. The questions you put are so general that my answers may mislead you."

He began to grow restless and fidgety.

"Although I am a believer in what *I* call animal magnetism and clairvoyance, I would not have you understand that I am a believer in a hundredth part of the stories told of others. What I see with my own eyes, and have had a fair opportunity of investigating and verifying, that I believe. What others tell me, I neither believe nor disbelieve. I wait for the proof. Suppose you state the case fairly."

"Do you believe that a clairvoyant can see hidden treasure in the earth, and that it would be safe to rely upon the assurances of such a person made in the magnetic sleep?"

"No."

"But suppose you had tried her?"

"*Her!* In what way?"

"By hiding a watch, for example, or a bit of gold, or a silver spoon, where nobody knew of it but yourself?"

"No; not even then."

"*No!* And why not, pray?"

"Simply because, judging by the experiments I have been able to make, I do not see any good reason for believing that, because a subject may tell us of what we ourselves know, or have heretofore known, which I admit very common, therefore she can tell me what I do not know and never did know. My notion is—but I maybe mistaken—that she sees with my eyes, hears with my ears, and remembers with my memory; and that she can do nothing more than reflect my mind while we are in communication."

"May be so; but the woman we are dealing with has actually pointed out the direction, and, at last, by a process of lining peculiar to herself, the actual position of what I had buried in the earth at a considerable distance, and without the knowledge or help of any living creature."

"Could she do this *always* and with *certainty*, and so that a third person might go to the treasure without help, on hearing her directions?"

"Why no, perhaps not; for that some few mistakes may have occurred, in the progress of our investigations, I am not disposed to deny."

"Probably. But, after all, were the directions given by her at any time, under any circumstances, definite and clear enough to justify a man of plain common sense in risking his reputation or money upon a third party's finding, without help, what you had concealed?"

Instead of answering my question, the poor fellow grew uneasy, and pale, and anxious; and, after considering awhile, and getting up and sitting down perhaps half a dozen times before he could make up his mind what to say, he told me a story—one of the most improbable I ever heard in my life—the leading features of which, nevertheless, I know to be true, and will vouch for as matters of fact.

There had been here, in Portland, for about six months, it appeared, a strange-looking, mysterious man—I give the facts, without pretending to give the words—who went by the name of Greenleaf. He was a sailor, and boarded with a man who kept a sailor boarding-house, and who, I am told, is still living here, by the name of Mellon. People had taken it into their heads that the stranger had something upon his mind, as he avoided conversation, took long walks by himself, and muttered all night long in his sleep. After a while, it began to be whispered about among the seafaring people that he was a pirate; and Mellon, his landlord, went so far as to acknowledge that he had his reasons for thinking so; although Greenleaf, on finding himself treated, and watched, and questioned more narrowly than he liked, managed to drop something about having sailed under the Brazilian flag. And, on being plied with liquor one day, with listeners about him, he went into some fuller particulars, which set them all agog. These, reaching the ears of Colonel Jones, led to an interview, from which he gathered that Greenleaf was one of a large crew commissioned by the Brazils in 1826; that, after cruising a long while in a latitude swarming with Spanish vessels of war, they got reduced to twenty-five men, all told. That one day they fell in with a large, heavily-laden ship, from which they took about three hundred and fifty thousand dollars, in gold and silver, and a massive gold cross, nearly two feet long, and weighing from fifteen to twenty pounds, belonging to a Spanish priest; but what they did with the crew and the passengers, or with the ship and the priest, did not appear. That, soon after getting their treasure aboard, they saw a large sail to windward, which they took to be a Spanish frigate; and, being satisfied with their booty, they altered their course, and steered for a desolate island near Guadaloupe, where, after taking out three hundred doubloons apiece, they landed, with the rest of the treasure packed in gun-cases, and hooped with iron; dug a hole in the earth and buried it; carefully removing the turf and replacing it, and carrying off all the dirt, and scattering it along the shore. That they took the bearings of certain natural objects, and marked the trees, and agreed among themselves, under oath, not to disturb the treasure till fifteen years had gone by, when it was to belong to the survivors. That, having done this, they steered for the Havana, and, after altering their craft to a fore-and-aft schooner, sold her, and shared the money. Being flush, and riotous, and quarrelsome, they soon got a-fighting among themselves; and, within a few months, by the help of the yellow fever, not less than twenty-three out of the whole twenty-five were buried, leaving only this Greenleaf and an old man, who went by the name of Thomas Taylor, and who had not been heard of for many years, and was now believed to be dead.

A fortune-teller was consulted, and put into a magnetic sleep, and, if the description they had painted of the man they were after could be depended on by her, they would find him, under another name, in a national ship on the East India station.

Here the Colonel began rubbing his hands again.

It appeared, moreover, that Taylor and Greenleaf had met more than once, and consulted together, and made two or three attempts to charter a vessel; but, being poor and among strangers, and afraid of trusting to other people—no matter why—they finally agreed to lie by till they were better off, and not be seen together till they should be able to undertake the enterprise without help from anybody.

"But," said Greenleaf. "I am tired of waiting. He may be dead for all I know He was an old man. At any rate, he is beyond my reach, out of hail; and so, d'ye see, if you'll rig us out a small schooner, of not more than seventy-five or eighty tons, I will go with you, and ask for no wages; and here's the landlord'll go, too, on the same lay; and, if you'll give me a third of what we find, I'll answer for Taylor, dead or alive, and you shall be welcome to the rest, and may do what you like with it."

"Would they consent to go *unarmed*?"

"Yes."

And all these facts being communicated to some of our people, and agreed to, a small schooner was chartered—the Napoleon, of ninety tons; Captain John Sawyer was put in master, and Watts, who had followed the sea forty years, and is now the keeper of Portland light, supercargo.

Not less than five, and it may be six, different voyages followed, one after the other, as fast as a vessel could be engaged and a crew got together; and, though nothing was "*realized*" but vexation, disappointment, and self-reproach, till the parties who had ventured upon the undertaking were almost ashamed to show their faces, there is not one of the whole to this hour, I verily believe, who does not stick to the faith and swear *it* was no *bubble*; and they are men of character and experience—men of business habits, cool and cautious in their calculations, and by no means given to chasing will-o'-the-wisps anywhere.

And now let me give the particulars that have since come to my knowledge, on the authority of those who were actually parties in the strange enterprise from first to last.

Before they sailed on their first voyage, they consulted a fortune teller by the name of Tarbox, who, without knowing their purpose, and while in a magnetic sleep, described the place, and the marks, and the treasure, even to the cross of gold, just as they had been described by Greenleaf himself. But she chilled their very blood at the time by whispering that, within two or three weeks at furthest, there would be a death among their number. Greenleaf made very light of the prediction at first, but grew serious, and, after a few days, gloomy, and refused to go. At last, however, he consented, and they had a very pleasant run to the edge of the Gulf Stream, latitude 38° and longitude 67°, when—but I must give this part of the story in the very language of Watts himself, a man still living, and worthy of entire confidence.

"We had been talking together pleasantly enough, and he seemed rather *chippur*. Only the night before, he had given me all the marks and bearings, and everything but the *distance*. He had never trusted anybody else in the same way, he said, but had rather taken a liking to me, and he kept back that one thing only that he might be safe, happen what must on the voyage. Well, we had been talking pleasantly together—it was about nine A.M., and the sea was running pretty high, and I had just turned to go aft, when something made me look round again, and I saw the poor fellow pitching head foremost over the side. He touched the water eight or ten feet from the vessel, but came up handsomely and struck out. He was a capital swimmer, and not at all frightened, so far as I could judge; for, if you'll believe me, squire, he never opened his mouth, but swum head and shoulders out of the water. At first, I thought he had jumped overboard; but afterwards, I made up my mind that he was knocked over by the leach of the foresail. I got hold of the gaff-topsail yard and run it under his arms, and threw a rope over him, and sung out 'Hold on, Greenleaf! hold on, and we'll save you yet.' But he took no notice of me, and steered right away from the vessel. I then called to Captain Sawyer that we would lower the boat, and asked him to jump in with me. There was a heavy sea on, and we let go the boat, and she filled; she *riz* once or twice, and then the stem and stern were ripped out, and the body went adrift; and when I looked again, there was nothing to be seen of poor Greenleaf. We ran for Guadaloupe and sold our cargo, and then for St. Thuras's, and then for the island where the money was buried. I offered to go ashore with Mellon, the Dutchman, though Captain Sawyer tried to discourage me."

"Well, you went ashore?"

"I did."

"And satisfied yourself?"

"I did."

"But how?"

"I found the marks and the trees, and a well sunk in the sand with a barrel in it; and I came to a place where the turf had settled, and a— and a—and, from what I saw, I believe the money was there just as much as I believe that I am talking with you now."

"You do!—then why the plague didn't you bring it home with you?"

"I'll tell you, squire. Fact is, we all agreed to go shears when the voyage was made up. Greenleaf was to have a third, the Dutchman a third, and Williams and M'Lellan a third, to be divided between Mr. C—Colonel Jones, I should say—Captain Sawyer, and myself. But, the moment Greenleaf was out of the way, the Dutchman grew sulky, and insisted on having his part—making two-thirds; and finally swore he would have it, or *die*. This we thought rather unreasonable; and, as I had the chart with me, and all the marks, while the Dutchman had nothing to help him in the search, I determined to lose myself on the island, feel round the shore a little, for my own satisfaction, and then steal off quietly, and try another voyage, with fewer partners. You understand, hey?"

"Well, my good friend, I don't ask you *how* you satisfied yourself; but I may as well acknowledge that I have understood from another owner—Colonel Jones himself—that you carried probes and other mining tools with you, such as you had been using on Jewell's Island for a long while; and that in pricking, where you found the turf a little sunk, you touched something about the size of a small tea-chest, and square, three feet below the surface?"

To this Watts made no answer.

"And here ended the first voyage, hey?"

"Yes."

"How many were made in all?"

"I made three trips, and Captain M'Lellan two—and it runs in my head there was another, but I am not sure. I returned from my third voyage on the 18th day of July, 1842, in the Grampus, a little schooner of about seventy-five tons."

"Perhaps you would have no objection to tell me something about the other voyages?"

"Well, squire, to tell you the truth, we didn't land at all on the second voyage. July 14th, we'd fell to leeward, and was beating up. I had been all night on the look-out—I was master that trip—and we had got far enough to bear up and run down under the lee of the island. We saw huts there, and twenty or thirty people, and we didn't much like their behavior. When they saw us, they ran down to the landing and took two boats and launched 'em. I offered to go ashore, if anybody would go with me. John Mac, he first agreed to it, but all the others refused; and then he said he would go if the others would. And then we steered for Portland Harbor."

"Well, and the third voyage?"

"That we made in the Grampus. Captain Josh Safford and Captain Bill Drinkwater went with us. We found two Spaniards upon the island. Their boats had gone to Porto Rico after provisions, they said. So Captain Safford, he gave them two muskets, with powder and ball, and they went off hunting goats. After this, I didn't consider myself justified in going ashore; and Captain Drinkwater complained a good deal of the liberty Safford took in supplying strangers with firearms. They might pop a fellow off at any time, you know, and nobody thereabouts would a ben the wiser."

"And here endeth the third voyage, hey?"

"Jess so."

"Do you happen to know anything about the other two?"

"Yes—for though I didn't go in the vessel, I knew pretty much all that happened. You see, Colonel Jones he went to work with the fortin-teller again; and he jest puts her to sleep, and tries her out and out, on Jewell's Island, where she found a skeleton fixed between two trees, and the walls of a hut, all grown over with large trees, and all the things he'd buried there; and then too, while we was at sea, she told him what we were doing, day by day, and they logged it all down: and when we got back and compared notes, we found it all true. Ah! he was a sharp one, I tell you! At last, he got her upon the track of Taylor. She found him in the East Indies, under another name, and shipped aboard one of our national ships. And so, what does he do but go to work and petition the Navy Department for Taylor's discharge, upon the ground that a grand estate had been left him—or, that he had large expectations, I forget which. He was very shy at first, and wouldn't acknowledge that he had ever gone by the name of Thomas Taylor. I dare say he had his reasons. But, after hunting him through hospitals, and navy yards, and sailor boarding-houses, and from ship to ship, the colonel he cornered him, and got him to say he would go with them. He told exactly the same story that Greenleaf did: I was taken sick, and couldn't go, and——-stop—I'm before my story, I believe—they made their voyage without him. They landed, dug trenches, and blistered their hands, and spent over two days in the search, while the schooner lay off and on, waiting for them: but they found nothing. After they got back, however, the colonel he had a meeting with the owners, and satisfied them all, in some way—I never knew how—that they had just reversed the bearings, and hadn't been near the place. How he knew, I can't say, for he had never been there, to my knowledge, and I happen to know that they must have been pretty near the spot, for they found a sort of a hillock that I remembered, and they told me all about the bearings, and they agreed with my chart."

"Well!—"

"Well, the next time they went, they took Taylor with them, and everything went on smoothly enough till one day, when the voyage was almost up, Taylor he said to Pearce—'Pearce,' said he, 'to-morrow, at this time, I shall be a rich man; and now,' says he, 'Mr. Pearce,' says he, 'I must have my letters.' Upon this, up steps John Mac, and says he, 'Taylor,' says he, 'when you want any letters, you'll have to come to me for them; and I shall have to put you upon allowance.' And then Taylor—he was an old man-o'-warsman, you see, and he couldn't get along without his grog—he jest ups and says—'that's enough, capt'n. You may haul aft the sheet, tack ship, and go home. I shall tell you nothing more. As soon as the money is safe—I see how 'tis—old Taylor'll have to go overboard.' And he stuck to what he said, though he went ashore with them, just to show them that he knew every point of the compass—for he told them where they would find a couple of holes in the ledge—and they found them there, just as he said; and the first thing they saw, there was Taylor away up on the top of a high mountain, smoking a pipe. He had always told them he knew how to get up there; but they never believed him, because they had all tried and couldn't fetch it."

"And he stuck to it, hey, and never told them anything more?"

"Jess so."

"And what became of Taylor? Is he living?"

"No; he died in the hospital at Bath not more than five years ago."

"And you still think the money was there?"

"Think!—I am sure of it."

"Do you believe it is there now?"

"Do I!—Certainly I do!"

Whereupon, all I have to say is—*Hurrah for bubbles!*

SONNET.—QUEEN OF SCOTS.

BY WM. ALEXANDER.

Within a castle's battlemented walls,

In crimsoned dungeon lay fair Scotia's queen:

Like drooping sorrow seemed she oft to lean

Her weary head. Pale, weeping memory recalls

The beaming joys of her life's early day,

Forever fled. Her spirit, palled with gloom,

Anticipates sweet rest but in the tomb—

White wingéd Faith, her guardian one, alway

There hovering nigh. 'Tis morn; dreams she no more;

On Fotheringay's black scaffold now she stands,

Clasping her cherished croslet in her hands,

Anon to die. Her fate the loves deplore;

The angel-loves, eke, waft her soul to heaven;

Her faults, her follies, to her faith forgiven.

THE PIONEER MOTHERS OF THE WEST.

BY MRS. E. F. ELLET.

MARY BLEDSOE.

The history of the early settlers of the West, a large portion of which has never been recorded in any published work, is full of personal adventure. No power of imagination could create materials more replete with romantic interest than their simple experience afforded. The early training of those hardy pioneers in their frontier life; the daring with Which they penetrated the wilderness, plunging into trackless forests, and encountering the savage tribes whose hunting-grounds they had invaded; and the sturdy perseverance with which they overcame all difficulties, compel our wondering admiration. But far less attention has been given to their exploits and sufferings than they deserve, because the accounts we have received are too vague and general; the picture is not brought near us, nor exhibited With life-like proportions and coloring; and our sympathy is denied to what we are unable to appreciate. It will, I am sure, be rendering a service to those interested in our American story to collect such traditionary information as can be fully relied upon, and thus show something of the daily life of those heroic adventurers.

The kindness of a descendant of one of those noble patriots who, after having won distinction in the struggle for Independence, sought new homes in the free and growing West,[1] enables me to present some brief notice of one family associated with the early history of Tennessee. The name of Bledsoe is distinguished among the pioneers of the Cumberland Valley. The brothers of this name— Englishmen by birth—were living in 1769 upon the extreme border of civilization, near Fort Chipel, a military post in Wyth County, Virginia. It was not long before they removed further into the wild, being probably the earliest pioneers in the valley of the Holston, in what is now called Sullivan County, Tennessee, a portion of country at that time supposed to be within the limits of Virginia. The Bledsoes, with the Shelbys, settled themselves about twelve miles above the Island Flats. The beauty of that mountainous region attracted others, who impelled by the same spirit of adventure, and pride in being the first to explore the wilderness, came to join them in establishing the colony. They cheerfully ventured their property and lives, enduring the severest privations in taking possession of their new homes, influenced by the love of independence, equality, and religious freedom. The most dearly-prized rights of man had been threatened in the oppressive system adopted by Great Britain towards her colonies; her agents and the colonial magistrates manifested all the insolence of authority; and individuals who had suffered from their aggressions bethought themselves of a country beyond the mountains, in the midst of primeval forests, where no laws existed save the law of Nature—no magistrate except those selected by themselves; where full liberty of conscience, of speech, and of action prevailed. Yet, almost in the first year of their settlement, they formed a written code of regulations by which they agreed to be governed; each man signing his name thereto. The pioneer settlements of the Holston and Watanga, formed by parties of emigrants from neighboring provinces, traveling together through the wilderness, were not, in their constitution, unlike those of New Haven and Hartford; but among them was no godly Hooker, no learned and heavenly-minded Haynes. As from the first, however, they were exposed to the continual depredations and assaults of their savage neighbors, who looked with jealous eyes upon the approach of the white men, and waged a war of extermination against them, it was perhaps well that there were among them few men of letters. The rifle and the axe, their only weapons of civilization, suited better the perils they encountered from the fierce and marauding Shawnees, Chickamangas, Creeks, and Cherokees, than would the brotherly address of William Penn, or the pious discourses of Roger Williams.

During the first year, not more than fifty families had crossed the mountains; but others came with each revolving season to reinforce the little settlement, until its population swelled to hundreds; increasing to thousands within ten or fifteen years, notwithstanding the frequent and terrible inroads upon their numbers of the Indian rifle and tomahawk. The dwelling-houses were forts, picketed, and flanked by block-houses, and the inhabitants, for mutual aid and protection, took up their residence in groups around different stations, within a short distance of one another.

Not long after the Bledsoes established themselves upon the banks of the Holston, Colonel Anthony Bledsoe, who was an excellent surveyor, was appointed clerk to the commissioners who ran the line dividing Virginia and North Carolina. Bledsoe had, before this, ascertained that Sullivan County was comprised within the boundaries of the latter province. In June, 1776, he was chosen by the inhabitants of the county to the command of the militia. The office imposed on him the dangerous duty of repelling the savages and defending the frontier. He had often to call out the militia and lead them to meet their Indian assailants, whom they would pursue to their villages through the recesses of the forest. The battle of Long Island, fought a few miles below his station, near the Island Flats, was one of the earliest and hardest fought battles known in the traditionary history of Tennessee. In June, 1776, more than seven hundred Indian warriors advanced upon the settlements on the Holston, with the avowed object of exterminating the white race through all their borders. Colonel Bledsoe, at the head of the militia, marched to meet them, and in the conflict which ensued was completely victorious; the Indians being routed, and leaving forty dead upon the field. This disastrous defeat for a time held them in check: but the spirit of savage hostility was invincible, and in the years following there was a constant succession of Indian troubles, in which Colonel Bledsoe was conspicuous for his bravery and services.

In 1779, Sullivan County having been recognized as a part of North Carolina, Governor Caswell appointed Anthony Bledsoe colonel, and Isaac Shelby lieutenant-colonel, of its military company. About the beginning of July of the following year, General Charles McDowell, who commanded a district east of the mountains, sent to Bledsoe a dispatch, giving him an account of the condition of the country. The surrender of Charleston had brought the State of South Carolina under British power; the people had been summoned to return to their allegiance, and resistance was ventured only by a few resolute spirits, determined to brave death rather than submit to the invader. The Whigs had fled into North Carolina, whence they returned as soon as they were able to oppose the enemy. Colonels Tarleton and Ferguson had advanced towards North Carolina at the head of their soldiery; and McDowell ordered Colonel Bledsoe to rally the militia of his county, and come forward in readiness to assist in repelling the invader's approach. Similar dispatches were sent to Colonel Sevier and to other officers, and the patriots were not slow in obeying the summons.

While the British Colonel Ferguson, under the orders of Cornwallis, was sweeping the country near the frontier, gathering the loyalists under his standard and driving back the Whigs, against whom fortune seemed to have decided, a resolute band was assembled for their succor far up among the mountains. From a population of five or six thousand, not more than twelve hundred of them fighting men, a body of near five hundred mountaineers, armed with rifles and clad in leathern hunting-shirts, was gathered. The anger of these sons of liberty had been stirred up by an insolent message received from Colonel Ferguson, that, "if they did not instantly lay down their arms, he would come over the mountains and whip their republicanism out of them;" and they were eager for an opportunity of showing what regard they paid to his threats.

At this juncture, Colonel Isaac Shelby returned from Kentucky, where he had been surveying land for the great company of land speculators headed by Henderson, Hart, and others. The young officer was betrothed to Miss Susan Hart, a belle celebrated among the western settlements at that period, and it was shrewdly suspected that his sudden return from the wilds of Kentucky was to be attributed to the attractions of that young lady; notwithstanding that due credit is given to the patriot, in recent biographical sketches, for an ardent wish to aid his countrymen in their struggle for liberty by his active services at the scene of conflict. On his arrival at Bledsoe's, it was a matter of choice with the colonel whether he should himself go forth and march at the head of the advancing army of volunteers, or yield the command to Shelby. It was necessary for one to remain behind, for the danger to the defenceless inhabitants of the country was even greater from the Indians than the British; and it was obvious that the ruthless savage would take immediate advantage of the departure of a large body of fighting men, to fall upon the enfeebled frontier. Shelby, on his part, insisted that it was the duty of Colonel Bledsoe, whose family, relatives, and defenceless neighbors looked to him for protection, to stay with the troops at home for the purpose of repelling the expected Indian assault. For himself, he urged, he had no family to guard, or who might mourn his loss, and it was better that he should advance with the troops to join McDowell. No one could tell where might be the post of danger and honor, at home or on the other side of the mountain. The arguments he used no doubt corresponded with his friend's own convictions, his sense of duty to his family, and of true regard to the welfare of his country; and the deliberation resulted in his relinquishment of the command to his junior officer. It was thus that the conscientious, though not ambitious, patriot lost the honor of commanding in one of the most distinguished actions of the Revolutionary War.

Colonel Shelby took the command of those gallant mountaineers who encountered the forces of Ferguson at King's Mountain on the 7th October, 1780. Three days after that splendid victory, Colonel Bledsoe received from him an official dispatch giving an account of the battle. The daughter of Colonel Bledsoe well remembers having heard this dispatch read by her father, though it has probably long since shared the fate of other valuable family papers.

When the hero of King's Mountain, wearing the victor's wreath, returned to his friends, he found that his betrothed had departed with her father for Kentucky, leaving for him no request to follow. Sarah, the above-mentioned daughter of Colonel Bledsoe, often rallied the young officer, who spent considerable time at her father's, upon this cruel desertion. He would reply by expressing much indignation at the treatment he had received at the hands of the fair coquette, and protesting that he would not follow her to Kentucky, nor ask her of her father; he would wait for little Sarah Bledsoe, a far prettier bird, he would aver, than the one that had flown away. The maiden, then some twelve or thirteen years of age, would laughingly return his bantering by saying he "had better wait, indeed, and see if he could win Miss Bledsoe who could not win Miss Hart." The arch damsel was not wholly in jest, for a youthful kinsman of the colonel—David Shelby, a lad of seventeen or eighteen, who had fought by his side at King's Mountain—had already gained her youthful affections. She remained true to this early love, though her lover was only a private soldier. And it may be well to record that, the gallant colonel who thus threatened infidelity to his, did actually, notwithstanding his protestations, go to Kentucky the following year, and was married to Miss Susan Hart, who made him a faithful and excellent wife.

During the whole of the trying period that intervened between the first settlement of east Tennessee and the close of the Revolutionary struggle, Colonel Bledsoe, with his brother and kinsmen, was almost incessantly engaged in the strife with their Indian foes, as well as in the laborious enterprise of subduing the forest, and converting the tangled wilds into the husbandman's fields of plenty. In these varied scenes of trouble and trial, of toil and danger, the men were aided and encouraged by the women. Mary Bledsoe, the colonel's wife, was a woman of remarkable energy, and noted for her independence both of thought and action. She never hesitated to expose herself to danger whenever she thought it her duty to brave it; and when Indian hostilities were most fierce, when their homes were frequently invaded by the murderous savage, and females struck down by the tomahawk or carried into captivity, she was foremost in urging her husband and friends to go forth and meet the foe, instead of striving to detain them for the protection of her own household. During this time of peril and watchfulness little attention could have been given to books, even had the pioneers possessed them; but the Bible, the Confession of Faith, and a few such works as Baxter's Call, Bunyan's Pilgrim's Progress, etc., were generally to be found in the library of every resident on the frontier.

About the close of the year 1779, Colonel Bledsoe and his brothers, with a few friends, crossed the Cumberland Mountains, descended into the valley of Cumberland River, and explored the beautiful region on its banks. Delighted with its shady woods, its herds of buffaloes, its rich and genial soil, and its salubrious climate, their report on their return induced many of the inhabitants of East Tennessee to resolve on seeking a new home in the Cumberland Valley. The Bledsoes did not remove their families thither until three years afterwards; but the idea of settling the valley originated with them; they were the first to explore it, and it was in consequence of their report and advice that the expedition was fitted out, under the direction of Captain (afterwards General) Robertson and Colonel John Donaldson, to establish the earliest colony in that part of the country. The account of this expedition, and the planting of the settlement, is contained in the memoir of "Sarah Buchanan," vol. iii. of "Women of the American Revolution."

The daughter of Colonel Bledsoe, from whose recollection Mr. Haynes has obtained most of the incidents recorded in these sketches, has in her possession letters that passed between her father and General Robertson, in which repeated allusions are made to the fact that to his suggestions and counsel was owing the first thought of emigration to the Cumberland Valley. In 1784, Anthony Bledsoe removed with his family to the new settlement of which he had thus been one of the founders. His brother, Colonel Isaac Bledsoe, had gone the year before. They took up their residence in what is now Sumner County, and established a fort or station at "Bledsoe's Lick"—now known as the Castalian Springs. The families being thus united, and the eldest daughter of Anthony married to David Shelby, the station became a rallying-point for an extensive district surrounding it. The Bledsoes were used to fighting with the Indians; they were men of well-known energy and courage, and their fort was the place to which the settlers looked for protection—the colonels being the acknowledged leaders of the pioneers in their neighborhood, and the terror, far and near, of the savage marauders. Anthony was also a member of the North Carolina Legislature from Sumner County.

From 1780 to 1794, or 1795, a continual warfare was kept up by the Creeks and Cherokees against the inhabitants of the valley. The history of this time would be a fearful record of scenes of bloody strife and atrocious barbarity. Several hundred persons fell victims to the ruthless foe, who spared neither age nor sex, and many women and children were carried far from their friends into hopeless captivity. The settlers were frequently robbed and their negro slaves taken away; in the course of a few years two thousand horses were stolen; their cattle and hogs were destroyed, their houses and barns burned, and their plantations laid waste. In consequence of these incursions, many of the inhabitants gathered together at the stations on the frontier, and established themselves under military rule for the protection of the interior settlements. During this desperate period, the pursuits of the farmer could not be abandoned; lands were to be surveyed and marked, and fields cleared and cultivated, by men who could not venture beyond their own doors without arms in their hands. The labors of those active and vigilant leaders, the Bledsoes, in supporting and defending the colony, were indefatigable. Nor was the heroic matron—the subject of this notice—less active in her appropriate sphere of action. Her family consisted of seven daughters and five sons, the eldest of whom, Sarah Shelby, was not more than eighteen when she came to Sumner. Mrs. Bledsoe was almost the only instructor of these children, the family being left to her sole charge while her husband was engaged in his toilsome duties, or harassed with the cares incident to an uninterrupted border warfare.

Too soon was this devoted wife and mother called upon to suffer a far deeper calamity than any she had yet experienced. On the night of the 20th July, 1788, the family were alarmed by hearing the horses and cattle running tumultuously around the station, as if suddenly frightened. Colonel Anthony Bledsoe, who was then at home, rose and went to the gate of the fort. As he opened it, he was shot down; the same ball killing an Irish servant, named Campbell, who had been long devotedly attached to him. The colonel did not expire immediately, but was carried back into the station, while preparations were made for defence. Aware of the near approach of death, Bledsoe's anxiety was to provide for the comfort of his family. He had surveyed large tracts of land, and had secured grants for several thousand acres, which constituted nearly his whole property. The law of North Carolina at that time gave all the lands to the sons, to the exclusion of the daughters. In consequence, should the colonel die without a will, his seven young daughters would be left destitute. In this hour of bitter trial, Mrs. Bledsoe's thoughts were not alone of her own sufferings, and the deadly peril that hung over them, but of the provision necessary for the helpless ones dependent on her care. She suggested to her wounded husband that a will should be immediately drawn up. It was done; and a portion of land was assigned to each of the seven daughters, who thus in after life had reason to remember with gratitude the presence of mind and affectionate care of their mother.

Her sufferings from Indian hostility were not terminated by this overwhelming stroke. A brief list of those who fell victims, among her family and kinsmen, may afford some idea of the trials she endured, and of the strength of character which enabled her to bear up, and to support others, under such terrible experiences. In January, 1793, her son Anthony, then seventeen years of age, while passing near the present site of Nashville, was shot through the body, and severely wounded, by a party of Indians in ambush. He was pursued to the gates of a neighboring fort. Not a month afterwards, her eldest son, Thomas, was also desperately wounded by the savages, and escaped with difficulty from their hands. Early in the following April, he was shot dead near his mother's house, and scalped by the murderous Indians. On the same day, Colonel

Isaac Bledsoe was killed and scalped by a party of about twenty Creek Indians, who beset him in the field, and cut off his retreat to his station, near at hand.

In April, 1794, Anthony, the son of Mrs. Bledsoe, and his cousin of the same name, were shot by a party of Indians, near the house of General Smith, on Drake Creek, ten miles from Gallatin. The lads were going to school, and were then on their way to visit Mrs. Sarah Shelby, the sister of Anthony, who lived on Station Camp Creek.

Some time afterwards, Mrs. Bledsoe herself was on the road from Bledsoe's Lick to the above-mentioned station, where the court of Sumner county was at that time held. Her object was to attend to some business connected with the estate of her late husband. She was escorted on her way by the celebrated Thomas S. Spencer, and Robert Jones. The party were waylaid and fired upon by a large body of Indians. Jones was severely wounded, and turning, rode rapidly back for about two miles; after which, he fell dead from his horse. The savages advanced boldly upon the others, intending to take them prisoners.

It was not consistent with Spencer's chivalrous character to attempt to save himself by leaving his companion to the mercy of the foe. Bidding her retreat as fast as possible, and encouraging her to keep her seat firmly, he protected her by following more slowly in her rear, with his trusty rifle in his hand. When the Indians in pursuit came too near, he would raise his weapon, as if to fire; and, as he was known to be an excellent marksman, the savages were not willing to encounter him, but hastened to the shelter of trees, while he continued his retreat. In this manner he kept them at bay for some miles, not firing a single shot—for he knew that his threatening had more effect—until Mrs. Bledsoe reached a station. Her life and his own were, on this occasion, saved by his prudence and presence of mind; for both would have been lost had he yielded to the temptation to fire.

This Spencer—for his gallantry and reckless daring, named "the Chevalier Bayard of Cumberland Valley"—was famed for his encounters with the Indians, by whom he had often been shot at, and wounded on more than one occasion. His proportions and strength were those of a giant, and the wonder-loving people were accustomed to tell marvelous stories concerning him. It was said that, at one time, being unarmed when attacked by the Indians, he reached into a tree, and, wrenching off a huge bough by main force, drove back his assailants with it. He lived for some years alone in Cumberland Valley—it is said, from 1776 to 1779—before a single white man had taken up his abode there; his dwelling being a large hollow tree, the roots of which still remain near Bledsoe's Lick. For one year—the tradition is—a man by the name of Holiday shared his retreat; but the hollow being not sufficiently spacious to accommodate two lodgers, they were under the necessity of separating, and Holiday departed to seek a home in the valley of the Kentucky River. But one difficulty arose; those dwellers in the primeval forest had but one knife between them! What, was to be done? for a knife was an article of indispensable necessity: it belonged to Spencer, and it would have been madness in the owner of such an article to part with it. He resolved to accompany Holiday part of the way on his journey, and went as far as Big Barren River. When about to turn back, Spencer's heart relented: he broke the blade of his knife in two, gave half to his friend, and with a light heart returned to his hollow tree. Not long after his gallant rescue of Mrs. Bledsoe, he was killed by a party of Indians, on the road from Nashville to Knoxville. For nearly twenty years he had been exposed to every variety of danger, and escaped them all; but his hour came at last; and the dust of the hermit and renowned warrior of Cumberland Valley now reposes on "Spencer's Hill," near the Crab Orchard, on the road between Nashville and Knoxville.

Bereaved of her husband, sons, and brother-in-law by the murderous savages, Mrs. Bledsoe was obliged alone to undertake, not only the charge of her husband's estate, but the care of the children, and their education and settlement in life. These duties were discharged with unwavering energy and Christian patience. Her religion had taught her fortitude under her unexampled distresses; and through all this trying period of her life, she exhibited a decision and firmness of character which bespoke no ordinary powers of intellect. Her mind, indeed, was of masculine strength, and she was remarkable for independence of thought and opinion. In person, she was attractive, being neither tall nor large, until advanced in life. Her hair was brown, her eyes gray and her complexion fair. Her useful life was closed in the autumn of 1808. The record of her worth, and of what she did and suffered, is an humble one, and may win little attention from the careless many, who regard not the memory of our "pilgrim mothers:" but the recollection of her gentle virtues has not yet faded from the hearts of her descendants; and those to whom they tell the story of her life will acknowledge her the worthy companion of those noble men to whom belongs the praise of having originated a new colony and built up a goodly state in the bosom of the forest. Their patriotic labors, their struggles with the surrounding savages, their efforts in the maintenance of the community they had founded—sealed, as they finally were, with their own blood, and the blood of their sons and relatives—will never be forgotten while the apprehension of what is noble, generous, and good survives in the hearts of their countrymen.

[1] Milton A. Haynes, Esq., of Tennessee, has furnished me with this and other accounts.

MORE GOSSIP ABOUT CHILDREN,

IN A FAMILIAR EPISTLE TO THE EDITOR.

BY LOUIS GAYLORD CLARK.

MY DEAR GODEY:—
I have not finished my gossip about children. I have a good deal yet to say touching their sensibilities, their nice discriminating sense, and the treatment which they too frequently receive from those who, although older than themselves, are in very many things not half so wise.

If you will take up Southey's Autobiography, written by himself (and his son), and recently published by my friends, the brothers Harper, you will find in the portion of Southey's early history, as recorded by himself, many striking examples of the keen susceptibility of childhood to outward and inward impressions, and of the deep feeling which underlies the apparently unthoughtful career of a young boy. It is a delightful opening of his whole heart to his reader. One sees with him the smallest object of nature about the home of his childhood; and it is impossible not to enter into all his feelings of little joys and poignant sorrows. I am not without the hope, therefore, that, in the few records which I am about to give you; partly of personal experience and partly of personal observation, I shall be able to enlist the attention of your readers; for, after all, each one of us, friend Godey, in our own more mature joys and sorrows, is but an epitome, so to speak, the great mass, who alike rejoice and grieve us.

I do not wish to exhibit anything like a spirit of egotism, and I assure you that I write with a gratified feeling that is a very wide remove from that selfish sentiment, when I tell you that I have received from very many parents, in different parts of the country, letters containing their "warm and grateful thanks" for the endeavor which I made, in a recent number of your magazine, to *create more confidence in childhood and youth*; to awaken, along with a "sense of *duty*"—that too frequent excuse for domestic tyranny—a feeling of generous forbearance for the trivial, venial faults of those whose hearts are just and tender, and whom "kindness wins when cruelty would repel." You must let me go on in my own way, and I will try to illustrate the truth and justice of my position.

I must go back to my very earliest schooldays. I doubt if I was more than five years old, a little boy in the country, when I was sent, with my twin-brother, to a summer "district school." It was kept by a "school-ma'am," a pleasant young woman of some twenty years of age. She was positively my *first love*. I am afraid I was an awkward scholar at first; but the enticing manner in which Mary —— (I grieve that only the faint *sound* of her unsyllabled name comes to me now from "the dark backward and abysm of Time") coaxed me through the alphabet and the words of one syllable; encouraged me to encounter those of two (the first of which I remember to this day, whenever the baker's bill for my children's daily bread is presented for audit); stimulated me to attack those of three; until, at the last, I was enabled to surmount that tallest of orthoëpical combinations, "*Mi-chi-li-mack-i-nack*", without a particle of fear; the enticing manner, I say, in which Mary —— accomplished all this, won my heart. She would stoop over and kiss me, on my low seat, when I was successful, and very pleasant were her "good words" to my ear. Bless your heart! I remember at this moment the feeling of her soft brown curls upon my cheek; and I would give almost anything now to see the first "certificate" of good conduct which I brought home, in her handwriting, to my mother, and which was kept for years among fans, bits of dried orange-peel, and sprigs of withered "caraway," in a corner of the bureau-"draw." All this came very vividly to me some time ago, when my own little boy brought home *his* first "school-ticket." He is not called, however—and I rejoice that he is not—to remember dear companions, who "bewept to the grave did go, with true-love showers."

"Oh, my mother! oh, my childhood!

Oh, my brother, now no more!

Oh, the years that push me onward,

Farther from that distant shore!"

But I am led away. I wanted merely to say that this "school-ma'am," from the simple *love* of her children, her little scholars, knew how to teach and how to *rule* them. I hope that not a few "school-ma'ams" will peruse this hastily-prepared gossip; and if they do, I trust they will remember, in the treatment of their little charges, that "the heart *must* leap kindly back to kindness." Why, my dear sir, I used to wait, in the summer afternoons, until all the little pupils had gone on before, so that I could place in the soft white hand of my school-mistress as confiding a little hand as any in which she may afterwards have placed her own, "in the full trust of love." I hope she found a husband good and true, and that she was blessed with what she loved, "wisely" and *not* "too well," children.

Now that I am on the subject of children at school, I wish to pursue the theme at a little greater length, and give you an incident or two in my farther experience.

It was not long after finishing our summer course with "school-ma'am" Mary ——, that we were transferred to a "man-school," kept in the district. And here I must go back, for just one moment, to say that, among the pleasantest things that I remember of that period, was the calling upon us in the morning, by the neighbors' children—and especially two little girls, new-comers from the "Black River country," then a vague terra incognita to us, yet only some thirty miles away—to accompany us to the school through the winter snow. How well I remember their knitted red-and-white woolen hoods, and the red-and-white complexions beaming with youth and high health beneath them! I think of Motherwell's going to school with his "dear Jenny Morrison," so touchingly described in his beautiful poem of that name, every time these scenes arise before me.

Well, at this "man-school" I first learned the lesson which I am about to illustrate. It is a lesson for parents, a lesson for instructors, and, I think, a lesson for children also. I remember names *here*, for one was almost burned into my brain for years afterwards.

There was something very imposing about "opening the school" on the first day of the winter session. The trustees of the same were present; a hard-headed old farmer, who sent long piles of "cord wood," beach, maple, bass-wood, and birch, out of his "own *pocket*," he used to say—and he might, with equal propriety, have said, "out of his own *head*," for surely *there* was no lack of "timber;" Deacon C——, an educated Puritan, who could spell, read, write, "punctify," and—"knew grammar," as he himself expressed it; a thin-faced doctor, whose horse was snorting at the door, and who sat, on that occasion, with his saddle-bags crossed on his knee, being in something of a hurry, expecting, I believe, an "addition" in the neighborhood, to the subject of my present gossip—at all events, I well remember peeping under the wrinkled leather-flaps of the "bags" and seeing a wooden cartridge-box, with holes for the death-dealing vials; and last, but not least, the town blacksmith, who was, in fact, worth all the other trustees put together, being a man of sound common sense, with something more than a sprinkling of useful education. Under the auspices of these trustees, this "man-school" was thus opened for the winter. "Now look you what befell."

For the first four or five days, our schoolmaster was quite amiable—or so at least he seemed. His "rules," and they were arbitrary enough, were given out on the second day; five scholars were "admonished" on the third; on the fourth, about a dozen were "warned," as the pedagogue termed it; and on the fifth, there was set up in the corner of an open closet, in plain sight of all the school, a bundle containing about a dozen birch switches, each some six feet long, and rendered lithe and tough by being tempered in the hot embers of the fire. These were to be the "ministers of justice;" and the portents of this "dreadful note of preparation" were amply fulfilled.

I had just begun to learn to write. My copy-book had four pages of "straight marks," so called, I suppose, because they are always crooked. I had also gone through "the hooks," up and down; but my hand was cramped; and I fear that my first "word-copy" was not as good as it ought to have been; but I "run out my tongue and tried" hard; and it makes me laugh, even now, to remember how I used to look along the line of "writing-scholars" on my bench, and see the rows of lolling tongues and moving heads over the long desk, mastering the first difficulties of chirography; some licking off "blots" of ink from their copy-books, others drawing in or dropping slowly out of the mouth, at each upward or downward "stroke" of the pen.

One morning, "the master" came behind me and overlooked my writing—

"Louis," said he, "if I see any more such writing as that, you'll repent it! I've *talked* to you long enough."

I replied that he had never, to my recollection, blamed me for writing badly but once; nor *had* he.

"Don't dare to contradict *me*, sir, but remember!" was his only reply.

From this moment, I could scarcely hold my pen aright, much less "write right." The master had a cat-like, stealthy tread, and I seemed all the while to feel him behind me; and while I was fearing this, and had reached the end of a line, there fell across my right hand a diagonal blow, from the fierce whip which was the tyrant's constant companion, that in a moment rose to a red and blue welt as large as my little finger, entirely across my hand. The pain was excruciating. I can recall the feeling as vividly, while I am tracing these lines, as I did the moment after the cruel blow was inflicted.

From that time forward I could not write at all; nor should I have pursued that branch of school-education at all that winter but that "the master's" cruelty soon led to his dismissal in deep disgrace. His floggings were almost incessant. His system was the "reign of terror," instead of that which "works by *love* and purifies the heart." His crowning act was feruling a little boy, as ingenuous and innocent-hearted a child as ever breathed, on the tops of his fingernails—a refinement of cruelty beyond all previous example. The little fellow's nails turned black and soon came off, and the "master" was turned away. I am not sorry to add that he was subsequently cowhided, while lying in a snow-bank, into which he had been "knocked" by an elder brother of the lad whom he had so cruelly treated, until he cried lustily for quarter, which was not *too* speedily granted.

But I come now to my illustration of the "law of kindness," in its effect upon myself. The successor to the pedagogue whom we have dismissed was a native of Connecticut. He was well educated, had a pleasant manner, and a smile of remarkable sweetness. I never saw him angry for a moment. On the first day he opened, he said to the assembled school that he wanted each scholar to consider him as *a friend*; that he desired nothing but their good; and that it was for the interest of *each one* of them that *all* should be careful to observe the few and simple rules which he should lay down for the government of the school. These he proclaimed; and, with one or two trivial exceptions, there was no infraction of them during the three winters in which he taught in our district.

Under his instruction, I was induced to resume my "experiences" in writing. I remember his coming to look over my shoulder to examine the first page of my copy-book: "Very well written," said he; "only *keep on* in that way, and you cannot fail to succeed." These encouraging words went straight to my heart. They were words of kindness, and their fruition was instantaneous. When the next two pages of my copy-book were accomplished, he came again to report upon my progress: "That is *well* done, Louis, quite *well*. You will soon require very little instruction from *me*. I am afraid you'll soon become to excel your teacher."

Gentle-hearted, sympathetic O—— M——! would that your "law of kindness" could be written upon the heart of every parent, and every guardian and instructor of the young throughout our great and happy country!

I have often wondered why it is that parents and guardians do not more frequently and more cordially *reciprocate the confidence of children*. How hard it is to convince a child that his father or mother can do wrong! Our little people are always our sturdiest defenders. They are loyal to the maxim that "the king can do no wrong;" and all the monarchs they know are their parents. I heard the other day, from the lips of a distinguished physician, formerly of New York, but now living in elegant retirement in a beautiful country town of Long Island, a touching illustration of the truth of this, with which I shall close this already too protracted article.

"I have had," said the doctor, "a good deal of experience, in the long practice of my profession in the city, that is more remarkable than anything recorded in the 'Diary of a London Physician.' It would be impossible for me to detail to you the hundredth part of the interesting and exciting things which I saw and heard. That which affected me most, of late years, was the case of a boy, not, I think, over twelve years of age. I first saw him in the hospital, whither, being poor and without parents, he had been brought to die.

"He was the most beautiful boy I ever beheld. He had that peculiar cast of countenance and complexion which we notice in those who are afflicted with frequent hemorrhage of the lungs. He was *very* beautiful! His brow was broad, fair, and intellectual; his eyes had the deep *interior* blue of the sky itself; his complexion was like the lily, tinted, just below the cheek-bone, with a hectic flush—

'As on consumption's waning cheek,

Mid ruin blooms the rose;'

and his hair, which was soft as floss silk, hung in luxuriant curls about his face. But oh, what an expression of deep melancholy his countenance wore! so remarkable that I felt certain that the fear of death had nothing to do with it. And I was right. Young as he was, he did not wish to live. He repeatedly said that death was what he most desired; and it was truly dreadful to hear one so young and so beautiful talk like this. 'Oh!' he would say, 'let me die! let me die! Don't *try* to save me; I *want* to die!' Nevertheless, he was most affectionate, and was extremely grateful for everything that I could do for his relief. I soon won his heart; but perceived, with pain, that his disease of body was nothing to his 'sickness of the soul,' which I could not heal. He leaned upon my bosom and wept, while at the same time he prayed for death. I have never seen one of his years who courted it so sincerely. I tried in every way to elicit from him what it was that rendered him so unhappy; but his lips were sealed, and he was like one who tried to turn his face from something which oppressed his spirit.

"It subsequently appeared that the father of this child was hanged for murder in B—— County, about two years before. It was the most cold-blooded homicide that had ever been known in that section of the country. The excitement raged high; and I recollect that the stake and the gallows vied with each other for the victim. The mob labored hard to get the man out of the jail, that they might wreak summary vengeance upon him by hanging him to the nearest tree. Nevertheless, law triumphed, and he was hanged. Justice held up her equal scales with satisfaction, and there was much trumpeting forth of this consummation, in which even the women, merciful, tender-hearted women, seemed to take delight.

"Perceiving the boy's life to be waning, I endeavored one day to turn his mind to religious subjects, apprehending no difficulty in one so young; but he always evaded the topic. I asked him if he had said his prayers. He replied—

"'*Once*, always—*now*, never.'

"This answer surprised me very much; and I endeavored gently to impress him with the fact that a more devout frame of mind would be becoming in him, and with the great necessity of his being prepared to die; but he remained silent.

"A few days afterwards, I asked him whether he would not permit me to send for the Rev. Dr. B———, a most kind man in sickness, who would be of the utmost service to him in his present situation. He declined firmly and positively. *Then* I determined to solve this mystery, and to understand this strange phase of character in a mere child. 'My dear boy,' said I, 'I implore you not to act in this manner. What can so have disturbed your young mind? You certainly believe there is a God, to whom you owe a debt of gratitude?'

"His eye kindled, and to my surprise, I might almost say horror, I heard from his young lips—

"'No, I don't *believe* that there is a God!'

"Yes, that little boy, young as he was, was an atheist; and he even reasoned in a logical manner for a mere child like him.

"'I cannot believe there is a God,' said he; 'for if there were a God, he must be merciful and just; and he never, *never*, NEVER could have permitted *my father*, who was innocent, to be hanged! Oh, my father! my father!' he exclaimed, passionately, burying his face in the pillow, and sobbing as if his heart would break.

"I was overcome by my own emotion; but all that I could say would not change his determination; he would have no minister of God beside him—no prayers by his bedside. I was unable, with all my endeavors, to apply any balm to his wounded heart.

"A few days after this, I called, as usual, in the morning, and at once saw very clearly that the little boy must soon depart.

"'Willie,' said I, 'I have got good news for you to-day. Do you think that you can bear to hear it?' for I really was at a loss how to break to him what I had to communicate.

"He assented, and listened with the deepest attention. I then informed him, as I best could, that, from circumstances which had recently come to light, it had been rendered certain that his father was entirely innocent of the crime for which he had suffered an ignominious death.

"I never shall forget the frenzy of emotion which he exhibited at this announcement. He uttered one scream—the blood rushed from his mouth—he leaned forward upon my bosom—and died!"

I leave this, friend Godey, with your readers. I had much more to say; and, perhaps, should it be desirable, I may hereafter give you one more chapter upon children.

SONG OF THE STARS.

E PLURIBUS UNUM—"*Many in One.*"

A NATIONAL SONG.

BY THOMAS S. DONOHO.

"E PLURIBUS UNUM!" The world, with delight,

Looks up to the starry blue banner of night,

In its many-blent glory rejoicing to see

AMERICA'S motto—the pride of the Free!

"E PLURIBUS UNUM!" Our standard for ever!

Woe, woe to the heart that would dare to dissever!

Shine, Liberty's Stars! your dominion increase—

A guide in the battle, a blessing in peace!

"E PLURIBUS UNUM!" And thus be, at last,

From land unto land our broad banner cast,

Till its Stars, like the stars of the sky, be unfurled,

In beauty and glory, embracing the world!

DEVELOUR.

A SEQUEL TO "THE NIEBELUNGEN."

BY PROFESSOR CHARLES E. BLUMENTHAL.

CHAPTER I.

The twenty-second of February, 1848, found Paris in a condition which only a Napoleon or a Washington could have controlled. The people felt and acted like a lion conscious that his fetters are corroded, yet still some what awed by the remembrance of the power which they once exercised over him.

Poverty and want, licentious habits and irreligious feeling, had contributed to bring about a ferocious discontent, which needed only the insidious and inflammatory articles spread broadcast over the land by designing men to fan into an insurrection.

Louis Philippe and his advisers exemplified the proverb *Quem Deus vuls perdere, prius dementas*, determined upon closing one of the best safety-valves of public discontent. The Reform Banquet had been prohibited, and *apparently* well-planned military preparations had been made to meet any possible hostile demonstrations, and to quench them at the outset. Troops paraded through the city in every direction, and every prominent place was occupied by squadrons of cavalry or squads of infantry. Nevertheless, soon after breakfast the people collected at various points, at first in small numbers; but gradually these swelled in size in proportion as they advanced to what appeared the centre to which all were attracted, the *Place de la Concorde*. Shouts, laughter, and merriment were heard from all quarters of the crowd, and the moving masses appeared more like a body of people going to some holiday amusement, than conspirators bent upon the overthrow of a government.

Just as a detached body of these was passing through the Rue de Burgoigne, a gentleman stepped out of one of the houses in that narrow street, and, partly led by curiosity and partly by his zeal for the popular cause, joined their ranks and advanced with them as far as the *Palais du Corps Legislatif*, where they were met by a troop of dragoons, who endeavored to disperse the crowd. Angry words were exchanged, and a few sabre blows fell among the crowd. One of the troopers, who seemed determined to check the advancing column, rode up to one who appeared to be a leader, and, raising his sword, exclaimed, "Back, or I'll cleave your skull!" But the youthful and athletic champion folded his arms, and, without the slightest discomposure, replied, "Coward! strike an unarmed man;—prove your courage!" The dragoon, without a reply, wheeled his horse, and rode to another part of the square. Just at that moment, another insolent trooper pressed his horse against the gentleman who had joined the crowd in the Rue de Burgoigne. The latter lifted his cane, and was about to chastise the soldier's insolence, when a man in a blouse and a slouched hat resembling the Mexican *sombrero*, arrested his arm, and whispered to him, "Do not strike! you are not in America: France is not as yet the place to resent the insolence of a soldier." Irritated at this unexpected interference, the gentleman endeavored to free his arm from the vice-like grasp of the new-comer, while he exclaimed, "Unhand me, sir! A free American is everywhere a freeman; and these soldiers shall not prevent me from proceeding and aiding the cause of an oppressed people." "Say rather a hungry people," replied the other; and then added with a smile, and in good English, "Has the quiet student of the Juniata been so soon transformed into a fierce revolutionary partisan? What would Captain Sanker say if he could see you thus turned into a hot-headed insurgent?"

"I have heard that voice before," replied the stranger. "Who are you, that you are so familiar with me and my friends?"

"One who will guide and advise you in the storm that is now brewing, which will soon overwhelm this goodly Nineveh, and in its course shake a throne to its foundation. But this is no place for explanations. Come—and on our way I will tell you who I am, and why I have mingled with this people, that know hardly, as yet, what they are about to do."

While saying this, he drew his companion into the Rue St. Dominique, and disentangled him thus from the crowd, which, now no longer opposed by the dragoons, moved onward towards the *Pont de la Concorde*. After they had crossed the Rue de Bac, they found the streets almost deserted, and then the man with the slouched hat turned to his companion and said—

"Has Mr. Filmot already forgotten the pic-nic on the banks of the Juniata, and the stranger guest whom he was good enough to invite to his house?"

Mr. Filmot, for it was he whom we found just now about to take an active part in the insurrection of the Parisian people, examined the features of his interlocutor closely and rather distrustfully, and finally exclaimed—"It cannot be that I see M. Develour in Paris and in this strange disguise? for only yesterday I received a letter from Mr. Karsh, in which he informs me that his friend is even now a sojourner at the court of the Emperor of Austria."

"That letter was dated more than a month ago," replied Mr. Develour. "I left the Prater city in the beginning of last month, and, it appears, have arrived just in time to prevent Mr. Filmot from committing a very imprudent act, which, by the way, you will recollect, was predicted to you in the magic mirror. Had you asked my advice before you left your native land to pursue your studies in the modern Nineveh, I would have counseled you to wait for a more propitious season. But, as soon as I heard of your presence in the city, I determined to watch over you and to warn you, if your enthusiasm should lead you to take too active a part in the deadly strife that awaits us here."

"You certainly do not think that a revolution is contemplated?" inquired Mr. Filmot.

"Come and see," replied Develour, while he continued his walk down the Rue St. Dominique. They then passed through the Rue St. Marguerite, and entered the Rue de Boucheries. About half way down the street they stopped before a mean-looking house. Develour rapped twice in quick succession at the door, and then, after a short interval, once more, and louder than before, immediately after the third rap, the door was partially and cautiously opened, and some one asked, in an under tone, "What do you want?"

"To see the man of the red mountain," replied Develour, in the same tone.

"What is your business?"

"To guide the boat."

"Where do you come from?"

"From the rough sea."

"And where do you wish to go to now?"

"To the still waters."

After this strange examination, the door was fully opened, and the doorkeeper said, "You may enter." But when he saw Filmot about to accompany Develour, he stopped him, and inquired by what right he expected to gain admission.

"By my invitation and introduction," said Develour, before Filmot had time to speak.

"That may not be," replied the doorkeeper. "No one has a right to introduce another, except those who have the word of the day."

"I have the word," said Develour; and then he whispered to him, "Not Martin, but Albert." After that he continued aloud, "Now go and announce me; we will wait here in the vestibule."

As soon as the doorkeeper, after carefully locking the door, had withdrawn into the interior of the house, Develour turned to his companion and asked him, "Have you ever come across an account of the Red Man, whom many believe to have exercised a great influence over the mind of Napoleon?"

"I have read some curious statements concerning an individual designated by that name; but have always considered them the inventions of an exuberant imagination," replied Filmot.

"You will soon have an opportunity to form a more correct opinion. I hope to have the pleasure, in a few minutes, to introduce you to him. As for his claims to—"

Before Develour had time to finish the sentence, a side door opened close by him, and a black boy, dressed in oriental costume, entered and bowed, with his hands crossed over his breast, and then said to Develour, in broken French, "The master told me to bid you welcome, and to conduct you into the parlor, where he will join you in a few minutes."

CHAPTER II.

Develour and Filmot followed their guide into a room fitted up in Eastern style. Divans made of cushions piled one upon another were placed all around the room, with small carpets spread before them. Light stands of beautiful arabesque work were tastefully distributed in various places, and in the centre played a small fountain fed by aromatic water. The lower part of the room contained a recess, the interior of which was concealed by a semi-transparent screen, which permitted the visitors to see that it was lit up by a flame proceeding from an urn. Heavy rich silk curtains, hung before the windows, excluded the glare of the sun, and were so arranged that the light in the room resembled that given by the moon when at its full. The atmosphere of the apartment was heavy with the perfumes of exotic plants and costly essences. The Moor requested them to be seated, and, again crossing his arms over his breast, he bowed and left the room.

As soon as the door had closed behind him, Develour said to Filmot: "It is reported that the Red Man appeared four times to Napoleon, and each time, in order to expostulate with him about the course he was pursuing; that, during each visit, he advised him what to do, and accompanied his advice with the promise of success, in case he would follow his counsel; and a threat of defeat if he persisted in disregarding it. The last visit which he paid to the Emperor was shortly before the battle of Waterloo. Montholon was in the antechamber, when the man with the red cloak entered his master's apartment. After renewed expostulations, he urged the Emperor to make an overture to the allied powers, and to promise that he would confine his claims to France, and pledge himself not to attempt conquest beyond the Rhine. When Napoleon, though half awed, rejected this advice with some irritation, his visitor rose, and solemnly predicted to him a signal defeat in the next great battle he would be compelled to fight; and, after that, an expulsion from his empire; and then left the room as abruptly as he had entered it.

"As soon as Napoleon had recovered from his surprise at the bold language and the sudden departure of his strange monitor, he hastened into the antechamber to call him back. But no one but Montholon was in the room, who, when questioned by the Emperor concerning the man who just left the cabinet, replied that, during the last half hour, no human being had passed through the antechamber, to seek ingress or egress. The sentinels on the staircases and at the gates were then examined, but they all declared that they had not seen any stranger pass their respective posts. Perplexed at this fruitless endeavor to recall the Red Man, Napoleon returned to his cabinet mystified and gloomy, disturbed by his self appointed monitor, and his predictions. Shortly afterwards, he fought the battle of Waterloo, and saw the prophecy fulfilled. He could never afterwards wholly divest himself of the belief that the Man in Red, as he was called by the officers, was an incarnation of his evil genius."

Before Develour had ceased speaking, a door opened in the the lower part of the room, and an old man advanced, with a slow but firm step, towards the two friends. The new-comer appeared to be a man of more than threescore years and ten, though not a falter in his step, not the slightest curvature of his lofty figure, evinced the approach of old age. He was a little above the middle height, lofty in his carriage, and dignified in all his movements. A high forehead gave an intellectual cast to a countenance habitually calm and commanding, and to which long flowing silver locks imparted the look of a patriarch ruler. He was dressed in a velvet morning-gown, which was confined around his waist by a broad belt of satin, upon which several formulas in Arabic were worked with silver thread; and on his feet he had slippers covered with letters similar to those on his belt. As soon as Develour became aware of his presence, he advanced to meet him, and said a few words in Arabic; then, introducing his friend, he continued, in English—"M. Delevert, permit me to make you acquainted with Mr. Filmot. Nothing but a desire to afford him the pleasure of knowing you, the friend and admirer of his countrymen and their institutions, could have induced me to absent myself from my post this morning."

"You are welcome, Mr. Filmot," said M. Delevour, "even at a time when our good city affords us little opportunity to make it a welcome place to a stranger."

"On the contrary," replied Filmot, "to an American and a true lover of liberty, it seems to hold out a very interesting spectacle, if what I have seen and heard to-day is a fair indication of what is to come."

"Ah," said M. Delevert, with a sad smile, "I fear that the philanthropic part of your expectations will be doomed to disappointment. But a fearful lesson will again be read to the oppressors of the people; a lesson which would have been more effectual if taught a year hence, but which circumstances prevent us to delay longer. In a few minutes, messengers will arrive from all parts of the city to report progress and the probable result. You will thus have an opportunity, if not otherwise engaged, to gain correct information of the insurrection in all quarters."

"Will you be displeased with me, my friend," said Develour, "if I tell you that not only of M. Delevert, but also of the Red Man have I spoken to Mr. Filmot; and I have even promised him that he shall hear from that mysterious being a detail of one of his visits to the emperors?"

"And can M. Develour think still of these things?" replied the old man, smiling good-humoredly. "How can they interest your friend Mr. Filmot—a citizen of a country where everything is worked for in a plain matter-of-fact way? What interest can *he* feel in the various means that were employed in an endeavor to make the military genius of the great warrior an instrument to bring about a permanent amelioration in the condition of the people?"

"The very mystery in which the whole seems enveloped," said Filmot, "would, in itself, be enough to interest me in it; particularly so now, when I have reason to believe myself in the presence of the chief actor—of him whom hitherto I have always regarded as the creation of an excited imagination."

"And why a creature of the imagination?" inquired M. Delevert. "Is it because I had it in my power to appear before the Emperor and to leave him unseen by other eyes? Or is it because of the truth of my predictions? Neither was impossible; neither required means beyond those which the scientific student of the book of nature, when properly instructed, can obtain. I resorted once even to a use of the utmost powers of nature, as far as they are known to me, in order to entice him, by a palpable proof of my ability to aid him, to promise that he would become an instrument in the hands of those who sought to usher in the dawn of a happier age, the age of true liberty, true equality; an age in which every man and *woman* would be able to feel, through the advantages of education and equal political and moral rights, unhampered by false prejudices, that all human beings were created free and equal. It was on the night before the battle of Austerlitz, when he, as was his frequent custom, visited the outpost, wrapped in his plain gray coat. At the hour of midnight, I presented myself before him, and offered to show him the plans of the enemy for the following day, on condition that he would not endeavor to meddle with anything he should see, except so far as necessary to obtain the promised information. He knew something of my ability to fulfil what I promised, and therefore did not doubt me, but gave his imperial word to fulfil his part of the compact. I then led him a few paces beyond the camp, and bade him be seated on a large stone, a fragment of an old heathen altar-stone. He had hardly taken his seat before a phantom-like being, in the garb of an officer in the Austrian army, was seen kneeling before him with a portfolio in his hand. Napoleon opened it, and found there all the information he desired. He complied strictly with his promise, and returned the portfolio as soon as he had taken his notes, and the officer disappeared like a vapor of the night. I then turned to the surprised monarch, and offered to repeat this specimen of my skill before every subsequent battle, if he would moderate his ambition and be content to be the first among his equals, the father of a wide-spread patriarchal family. But he angrily refused to listen to such a proposal, and, having somewhat recovered from his surprise, called for his guards to seize me. Fool! He stood upon a spot where I could have killed him without the danger of its ever becoming known to any one. While he turned to look for his myrmidons, the ground opened beneath my feet, and I disappeared before he had time to see by what means I escaped.

"Twice have I thus visited Alexander of Russia, but with like results. Fate has decreed it otherwise. Freedom cannot come to mankind from a throne. But, from what my friend Develour has told you already, you may be astonished that we should have engaged, and still engage, in fruitless efforts, when we have gained from nature powers by which the sage is able to glance at the decrees. Alas! this earthly frame loads us with physical clogs that weigh us down, and throw frequently a film before the eyes which make even the clearest dim and short-sighted."'

Here they were interrupted by a few raps at the inner door, which M. Delevert seemed to count with great attention; and then rising from his seat, he continued, without any change in the tone of his voice—

"The reporters are coming in. If you will accompany me to my reception-room, you will have an opportunity, shared by no other foreigner, to become acquainted with the mainsprings of this revolution; for such I am determined it shall become. Alas! would that it were of a nature to be the last one! But their haste prevents that altogether. Come, they are waiting for me."

(To be continued.)

THE MOURNER'S LAMENT.

BY PARK BENJAMIN.

The night-breeze fans my faded cheek,

And lifts my damp and flowing hair—

And lo! methinks sweet voices speak,

Like harp-strings to the viewless air;

While in the sky's unmeasured scroll,

The burning stars forever roll,

Changeless as heaven, and deeply bright—

Fair emblems of a world of light!

Oh, bathe my temples with thy dew,

Sweet Evening, dearest parent mild,

And from thy curtained home of blue,

Bend calmly o'er thy tearful child:

For, when I feel, so soft and bland,

The pressure of thy tender hand,

I dream I rest in peace the while,

Cradled beneath my mother's smile.

That mother sleeps! the snow-white shroud

Enfolds her stainless bosom now,

And, like bright hues on some pale cloud,

Rose-leaves were woven round her brow.

I wreathed them that to heaven's pure bowers,

Surrounded with the breath of flowers,

Her soul might soar through mists divine,

Like incense from a holy shrine.

How changed my being! moments sweep

Down, down the eternal gulf of Time;

And we, like gilded bubbles, keep

Our course amid their waves sublime,

Till, mingled with the foam and spray,

We flash our lives of joy away;

Or, drifting on through Sorrow's shades,

Sink as a gleam of starlight fades.

Alone! alone! I'm left alone—

A creature born to grieve and die;

But, while upon Night's sapphire throne,

In yonder broad and glorious sky,

I gaze in sadness—lo! I feel

A vision of the future steal

Across my sight, like some faint ray

That glimmers from the fount of day.

OTHELLO TO IAGO.

BY R.T. CONRAD.

Accursed be thy life! Darkness thy day!

Time, a slow agony; a poison, love;

Wild fears about thee, wan despair above!

Crush'd hopes, like withered leaves, bestrew thy way!

Nothing that lives lov'st thou; nothing that lives

Loves thee. The drops that fall from Hecla's snow

'Neath the slant sun, are warmer than the flow

Of thy chill'd heart. Thine be the bolt that rives!

Be there no heaven to thee; the sky a pall;

The earth a rack; the air consuming fire;

The sleep of death and dust thy sole desire—

Life's throb a torture, and life's thought a thrall:

And at the judgment may thy false soul be,

And, 'neath the blasting blaze of light, *meet me!*

PERSONS AND PICTURES FROM THE HISTORY OF ENGLAND.

BY HENRY WILLIAM HERBERT.

NO. I.—SIR WALTER RALEIGH AND HIS WIFE.

It is commonly said, and appears generally to be believed by superficial students of history, that with the reigns of the Plantagenets, with the Edwards and the Henrys of the fifteenth century, the age of chivalry was ended, the spirit of romance became extinct. To those, however, who have looked carefully into the annals of the long and glorious reign of the great Elizabeth, it becomes evident that, so far from having passed away with the tilt and tournament, with the complete suits of knightly armor, and the perilous feats of knight-errantry, the fire of chivalrous courtesy and chivalrous adventure never blazed more brightly, than at the very moment when it was about to expire amid the pedantry and cowardice, the low gluttony and shameless drunkenness, which disgraced the accession of the first James to the throne of England. Nor will the brightest and most glorious names of fabulous or historic chivalry, the Tancreds and Godfreys of the crusades, the Oliviers and Rolands of the court of Charlemagne, the Old Campeador of old Castile, or the *preux* Bayard of France, that *chevalier sans peur et sans reproche*, exceed the lustre which encircles, to this day, the characters of Essex, Howard, Philip Sidney, Drake, Hawkins, Frobisher, and Walter Raleigh.

It was full time that, at this period, maritime adventure had superseded the career of the barded war-horse, and the brunt of the leveled spear; and that to foray on the Spanish colonies, beyond the line, where, it was said, truce or peace never came; to tempt the perils of the tropical seas in search of the Eldorado, or the Fountain of Health and Youth, in the fabled and magical realms of central Florida; and to colonize the forest shores of the virgin wildernesses of the west, was now paramount in the ardent minds of England's martial youth, to the desire of obtaining distinction in the bloody battle-fields of the Low Countries, or in the fierce religious wars of Hungary and Bohemia. And of these hot spirits, the most ardent, the most adventurous, the foremost in everything that savored of romance or gallantry, was the world-renowned Sir Walter Raleigh.

Born of an honorable and ancient family in Devonshire, he early came to London, in order to push his fortunes, as was the custom in those days with the cadets of illustrious families whose worldly wealth was unequal to their birth and station, by the chances of court favor, or the readier advancement of the sword. At this period, Elizabeth was desirous of lending assistance to the French Huguenots, who had been recently defeated in the bloody battle of Jarnac, and who seemed to be in considerable peril of being utterly overpowered by their cruel and relentless enemies the Guises; while she was at the same time wholly disinclined to involve England in actual strife, by regular and declared hostilities.

She gave permission, therefore, to Henry Champernon to raise a regiment of gentlemen volunteers, and to transport them into France. In the number of these, young Walter Raleigh enrolled, and thenceforth his career may be said to have commenced; for from that time scarce a desperate or glorious adventure was essayed, either by sea or land, in which he was not a participator. In this, his first great school of military valor and distinction, he served with so much spirit, and such display of gallantry and aptitude for arms, that he immediately attracted attention, and, on his return to England in 1570, after the pacification, and renewal of the edicts for liberty of conscience, found himself at once a marked man.

It seems that, about this time, in connection with Nicholas Blount and others, who afterward attained to both rank and eminence, Raleigh attached himself to the Earl of Essex, who at that time disputed with Leicester the favors, if not the affection, of Elizabeth; and, while in his suite, had the fortune to attract the notice of that princess by the handsomeness of his figure and the gallantry of his attire; she, like her father, Henry, being quick to observe and apt to admire those who were eminently gifted with the thews and sinews of a man.

A strangely romantic incident was connected with his first rise in the favor of the Virgin Queen, which is so vigorously and brilliantly described by another and even more renowned Sir Walter in his splendid romance of Kenilworth, that it shames us to attempt it with our far inferior pen; but it is so characteristic of the man and of the times that it may not be passed over in silence.

Being sent once on a mission—so runs the tale—by his lord to the queen, at Greenwich, he arrived just as she was issuing in state from the palace to take her barge, which lay manned and ready at the stairs. Repulsed by the gentlemen pensioners, and refused access to her majesty until after her return from the excursion, the young esquire stood aloof, to observe the passing of the pageant; and, seeing the queen pause and hesitate on the brink of a pool of rain-water which intersected her path, no convenience being at hand wherewith to bridge it, took off his crimson cloak, handsomely laid down with gold lace, his only courtlike garment, fell on one knee, and with doffed cap and downcast eyes threw it over the puddle, so that the queen passed across dry shod, and swore by God's life, her favorite oath, that there was chivalry and manhood still in England.

Immediately thereafter, he was summoned to be a member of the royal household, and was retained about the person of the queen, who condescended to acts of much familiarity, jesting, capping verses, and playing at the court games of the day with him, not a little, it is believed, to the chagrin of the haughty and unworthy favorite, Dudley, Earl of Leicester.

It does not appear, however, that, although she might coquet with Raleigh, to gratify her own love of admiration, and to enjoy the charms of his rich and fiery eloquence and versatile wit, though she might advance him in his career of arms, and even stimulate his vaulting ambition to deeds of yet wilder emprise, she ever esteemed

Raleigh as he deserved to be esteemed, or penetrated the depths of his imaginative and creative genius, much less beloved him personally, as she did the vain and petty ambitious Leicester, or the high-spirited, the valorous, the hapless Essex.

Another anecdote is related of this period, which will serve in no small degree to illustrate this trait of Elizabeth's strangely-mingled nature. Watching with the ladies of her court, in the gardens of one of her royal residences, as was her jealous and suspicious usage, the movements of her young courtier, when he either believed, or affected to believe himself unobserved, she saw him write a line on a pane of glass in a garden pavilion with a diamond ring, which, on inspecting it subsequently to his departure, she found to read in this wise:—

"Fain would I climb, but that I fear to fall—"

the sentence, or the distich rather, being thus left unfinished, when, with her royal hand, she added the second line—no slight encouragement to so keen and fiery a temperament as that of him for whom she wrote, when given him from such a source—

"If thy heart fail thee, do not climb at all."

But his heart never failed him—not in the desperate strife with the Invincible Armada—not when he discovered and won for the English crown the wild shores of the tropical Guiana—not when he sailed the first far up the mighty Orinoco—not when, in after days, he stormed Cadiz, outdoing even the daring deeds of emulous and glorious—not when the favor of Elizabeth was forfeited—not in the long years of irksome, solitary, heart-breaking imprisonment, endured at the hands of that base, soulless despot, the first James of England—not at his parting from his beloved and lovely wife—not on the scaffold, where he died as he had lived, a dauntless, chivalrous, high-minded English gentleman.

The greatest error of his life was his pertinacious hostility to Essex, originating in the jealousy of that brave, but rash and headstrong leader, who disgraced and suspended him after the taking of Fayal, a circumstance which he never forgave or forgot—an error which ultimately cost him his own life, since it alienated from him the affections of the English people, and rendered them pitiless to him in his own extremity.

But his greatest crime, in the eyes of Elizabeth, the crime which lost him her good graces for ever, and neutralized all his services on the flood and in the field, rendering ineffective even the strange letter which he addressed to his friend, Sir Robert Cecil, and which was doubtless shown to the queen, although it failed to move her implacable and iron heart, was his marriage, early in life, to the beautiful and charming Elizabeth Throgmorton. The letter to which I have alluded is so curious that I cannot refrain from quoting it entire, as a most singular illustration of the habits of that age of chivalry, and of the character of that strange compound, Elizabeth, who, to the "heart of a man, and that man a king of England," to quote her own eloquent and noble diction, added the vanity and conceit of the weakest and most frivolous of womankind, and who, at the age of sixty years, chose to be addressed as a Diana and a Venus, a nymph, a goddess, and an angel.

> "My heart," he wrote, "was never till this day, that I hear the queen goes away so far off, whom I have followed so many years, with so great love and desire, in so many journeys, and am now left behind here, in a dark prison all alone. While she was yet near at hand, that I might hear of her once in two or three days, my sorrows were the less; but even now my heart is cast into the depth of all misery. I, that was wont to behold her riding like Alexander, hunting like Diana, walking like Venus, the gentle wind blowing her fair hair about her pure cheeks like a nymph, sometimes sitting in the shade like a goddess, sometimes singing like an angel, sometimes playing like Orpheus. Behold the sorrow of this world! Once a miss has

bereaved me of all. Oh! glory, that only shineth in misfortune, what is become of thy assurance? All wounds have scars but that of fantasy: all affections their relentings but that of womankind. Who is the judge of friendship but adversity? or when is grace witnessed but in offences? There was no divinity but by reason of compassion; for revenges are brutish and mortal. All those times past, the loves, the sighs, the sorrows, the desires, cannot they weigh down one frail misfortune? Cannot one drop of gall be his in so great heaps of sweetness? I may then conclude, '*spes et fortuna valete;*' she is gone in whom I trusted, and of me hath not one thought of mercy, nor any respect of that which was. Do with me now, therefore, what you list. I am more weary of life than they are desirous that I should perish; which, if it had been for her, as it is by her, I had been too happily born."

It is singular enough that such a letter should have been written, under any circumstances, by a middle-aged courtier to an aged queen; but it becomes far more remarkable and extraordinary when we know that the life of Raleigh was not so much as threatened at the time when he wrote; and, so far had either of the parties ever been from entertaining any such affection the one for the other as could alone, according to modern ideas, justify such fervor of language, that Elizabeth was at that time pining with frustrated affection and vain remorse for the death of her beloved Essex; a remorse which, in the end, broke a heart which had defied all machinations of murdereous conspiracies, all menaces, all overtures of the most powerful and martial princes to sway it from its stately and impressive magnanimity; while Raleigh was possessed by the most perfect and enduring affection to the almost perfect woman whom he held it his proudest trophy to have wedded, and who justified his entire devotion by her love unmoved through good or ill report, and proved to the utmost in the dungeon and on the scaffold—the love of a pure, high-minded, trusting woman, confident, and fearless, and faithful to the end.

It does not appear that Raleigh suspected the true cause of Elizabeth's alienation from so good and great a servant: perhaps no one man of the many whom for the like cause she neglected, disgraced, persecuted, knew that the cause existed in the fact of their having taken to themselves partners of life and happiness—a solace which she sacrificed to the sterile honors of an undivided crown—of their enjoying the bliss and perfect contentment of a happy wedded life, while she, who would fain have enjoyed the like, could she have done so without the loan of some portion of her independent and undivided authority, was compelled, by her own jealousy of power and obstinacy of will, to pine in lonely and unloved virginity.

Yet such was doubtless the cause of his decline in the royal favor, which he never, in after days, regained; for, after Essex was dead by her award and deed, Elizabeth, in her furious and lion-like remorse, visited his death upon the heads of all those who had been his enemies in life, or counseled her against him, even when he was in arms against her crown; nor forgave them any more than she forgave herself, who died literally broken-hearted, the most lamentable and disastrous of women, if the proudest and most fortunate queens, in the heyday of her fortunes, when she had raised her England to that proud and pre-eminent station above rather than among the states of Europe, from which she never declined, save for a brief space under her successors, those weakest and wickedest of English kings, the ominous and ill-starred Stuarts, and which she still maintains in her hale and superb old age, savoring, after nearly nine centuries of increasing might and scarcely interrupted rule, in no respect of decrepitude or decay.

Her greatest crime was the death of Mary Stuart; her greatest misfortune, the death of Essex; her greatest shame, the disgrace of Walter Raleigh. But with all her crimes, all her misfortunes, all her shame, she was a great woman, and a glorious queen, and in both qualities peculiarly and distinctively English. The stay and bulwark of her country's freedom and religion, she lived and died possessed of that rarest and most divine gift to princes, her people's unmixed love and veneration.

She died in an ill day, and was succeeded by one in all respects her opposite: a coward, a pedant, a knave, a tyrant, a mean, base, beastly sensualist—a bad man, devoid even of a bad man's one redeeming virtue, physical courage—a bad weak man with the heart of a worse and weaker woman—a man with all the vices of the brute creation, without one of their virtues. His instincts and impulses were all vile and low, crafty and cruel; his principles, if his rules of action, which were all founded on cheatery and subtle craft, can be called principles, were yet baser than his instinctive impulses.

He is the only man I know, recorded in history, who is solely odious, contemptible, and bestial, without one redeeming trait, one feature of mind or body that can preserve him from utter and absolute detestation and damnation of all honorable and manly minds.

He is the only king of whom, from his cradle to his grave, no one good deed, no generous, or bold, or holy, or ambitious, much less patriotic or aspiring, thought or action is related.

His soul was akin to the mud, of which his body was framed—to the slime of loathsome and beastly debauchery, in which he wallowed habitually with his court and the ladies of his court, and his queen at their head, and could no more have soared heavenward than the garbage-battened vulture could have soared to the noble falcon's pitch and pride of place.

This beast,[1] for I cannot bring myself to write him man or king, with the usual hatred and jealousy of low foul minds towards everything noble and superior, early conceived a hatred for the gallant and great Sir Walter Raleigh, whose enterprise and adventure he had just intellect enough to comprehend so far as to fear them, but of whose patriotism, chivalry, innate nobility of soul, romantic daring, splendid imagination, and vast literary conceptions—being utterly unconscious himself of such emotions—he was no more capable of forming a conception, than is the burrowing mole of appreciating the flight of the soaring eagle.

So early as the second year of his reign, he contrived to have this great discoverer and gallant soldier—to whom Virginia is indebted for the honor of being the first English colony, Jamestown having been settled in 1606, whereas the Puritans landed on the rock of Plymouth no earlier than 1620, and to whom North Carolina has done honor creditable to herself in naming her capital after him, the first English colonist—arraigned on a false charge of conspiracy in the case of Arabella Stuart, a young lady as virtuous and more unfortunate than sweet Jane Grey, whose treatment by James would alone have been enough to stamp him with eternal infamy, and for whose history we refer our readers to the fine novel by Mr. James on this subject.

At this time, Raleigh was unpopular in England, on account of his supposed complicity in the death of Essex; and, on the strength of this unpopularity, he was arraigned, on the single *written* testimony of one Cobham, a pardoned convict of the same conspiracy, which testimony he afterwards retracted, and then again retracted the retractation, and without one concurring circumstance, without being confronted with the prisoner, after shameless persecution from Sir Edward Coke, the great lawyer, then attorney-general, was found guilty by the jury, and sentenced, contrary to all equity and justice, to the capital penalties of high treason.

From this year, 1604, until 1618, a period of nearly fourteen years, not daring to put him at that time to death, he caused him to be confined strictly in the Tower, a cruel punishment for so quick and active a spirit, which he probably expected would speedily release him by a natural death from one whom he regarded as a dangerous and resolute foe, whom he dared neither openly to dispatch nor honorably to release from unmerited and arbitrary confinement.

But his cruel anticipations were signally frustrated by the noble constancy, and calm, self-sustained intrepidity of the noble prisoner, who, to borrow the words of his detractor, Hume, "being educated amid naval and military enterprises, had surpassed, in the pursuits of literature, even those of the most recluse and sedentary lives."

Supported and consoled by his exemplary and excellent wife, he was enabled to entertain the irksome days and nights of his solitary imprisonment by the composition of a work, which, if deficient in the points which are now, in the advanced state of human sciences, considered essential to a great literary creation, is, as regarded under the circumstances of its conception and execution, one of the greatest exploits of human ingenuity and human industry—"The History of the World, by Sir Walter Raleigh."

It was during his imprisonment also that he projected the colonization of Jamestown, which was carried out in 1606, at his instigation, by the Bristol Company, of which he was a member. This colony, though it was twice deserted, was in the end successful, and in it was born the first child, Virginia Dare by name, of that Anglo-Saxon race which has since conquered a continent, and surpassed, in the nonage of its republican sway, the maturity of mighty nations.

In 1618, induced by the promises of Raleigh to put the English crown in possession of a gold mine which he asserted, and probably believed he had discovered in Guiana, James, whose avidity always conquered his resentments, and who, like Faustus, would have sold his soul—had he had one to sell—for gold, released him, and, granting him, as he asserted, an unconditional pardon—but, as James and his counselors maintain, one conditional on fresh discoveries, sent him out at the head of twelve armed vessels.

What follows is obscure; but it appears that Raleigh, failing to discover the mines, attacked and plundered the little town of St. Thomas, which the Spaniards had built on the territories of Guiana, which Raleigh had acquired three-and-twenty years before for the English crown, and which James, with his wonted pusillanimity, had allowed the Spaniards to occupy, without so much as a remonstrance.

This conduct of Raleigh must be admitted unjustifiable, as Spain and England were then in a state of profound peace; and the plea that truce or peace with Spain never crossed the line, though popular in England in those days of Spanish aggression and Romish intolerance, cannot for a moment stand the test either of reason or of law.

Falling into suspicion with his comrades, Sir Walter was brought home in irons, and delivered into the hands of the pitiless and rancorous king, who resolved to destroy him—yet, dreading to awaken popular indignation by delivering him up to Spain, caused to revive the ancient sentence, which had never been set aside by a formal pardon, and cruelly and unjustly executed him on that spot, so consecrated by the blood of noble patriots and holy martyrs, the dark and gory scaffold of Tower Hill.

And here, in conclusion, I can do no better than to quote from an anonymous writer in a recent English magazine, the following brief tribute to his high qualities, and sad doom, accompanied by his last exquisite letter to his wife.

"His mind was indeed of no common order. With him, the wonders of earth and the dispensations of heaven were alike welcome; his discoveries at sea, his adventures abroad, his attacks on the colonies of Spain, were all arenas of glory to him—but he was infinitely happier by his own fireside, in recalling the spirits of the great in the history of his country—nay, was even more contented in the gloom of his ill-deserved prison, with the volume of genius or the book of life before him, than in the most animating successes of the battle-field.

"The event which clouded his prosperity and destroyed his influence with the queen—his marriage with Elizabeth Throgmorton—was the one upon which he most prided himself; and justly, too—for, if ever woman was created the companion, the solace of man—if ever wife was deemed the dearest thing of earth to which earth clings, that woman was his wife. Not merely in the smiles of the court did her smiles make a world of sunshine to her Raleigh; not merely when the destruction of the Armada made her husband's name glorious; not merely when his successes and his discoveries on the ocean made his presence longed for at the palace, did she interweave her best affections with the lord of her heart. It was in the hour of adversity she became his dearest companion, his 'ministering angel;' and when the gloomy walls of the accursed Tower held all her empire of love, how proudly she owned her sovereignty! Not even before the feet of her haughty mistress, in her prayerful entreaties for her dear Walter's life, did she so eminently shine forth in all the majesty of feminine excellence as when she guided his counsels in the dungeon, and nerved his mind to the trials of the scaffold, where, in his manly fortitude, his noble self-reliance, the people, who mingled their tears with his triumph, saw how much the patriot was indebted to the woman.

"Were there no other language but that of simple, honest affection, what a world of poetry would remain to us in the universe of love! You may be excited to sorrow for his fate by recalling the varied incidents of his attractive life: you may mourn over the ruins of his chapel at his native village: you may weep over the fatal result of his ill-starred patriotism: you may glow over his successes in the field or on the wave: your lip may curl with scorn at the miserable jealousy of Elizabeth: your eye may kindle with wrath at the pitiful tyranny of James—but how will your sympathies be so awakened as by reading his last, simple, touching letter to his wife.

> "'You receive, my dear wife, my last words, in these my last lines. My love, I send you that you may keep it when I am dead; and my counsel, that you may remember it when I am no more. I would not with my will present you with sorrows, dear Bess—let them go to the grave with me and be buried in the dust—and, seeing that it is not the will of God that I should see you any more, bear my destruction patiently, and with a heart like yourself.

"'First—I send you all the thanks which my heart can conceive, or my words express, for your many travels and cares for me, which, though they have not taken effect as you wished, yet my debt to you is not the less; but pay it I never shall in this world.

"'Secondly—I beseech you, for the love you bear me living, that you do not hide yourself many days, but by your travels seek to help my miserable fortunes and the right of your poor child—your mourning cannot avail me that am dust—for I am no more yours, nor you mine—death hath cut us asunder, and God hath divided me from the world, and you from me.

"'I cannot write much. God knows how hardly I steal this time when all sleep. Beg my dead body, which, when living, was denied you, and lay it by our father and mother—I can say no more—time and death call me away;—the everlasting God—the powerful, infinite, and inscrutable God, who is goodness itself, the true light and life, keep you and yours, and have mercy upon me, and forgive my persecutors and false accusers, and send us to meet in his glorious kingdom.

"My dear wife—farewell! Bless my boy—pray for me, and let the true God hold you both in his arms.

"'Yours, that was; but now, not mine own,

"'WALTER RALEIGH.'"

"Thus a few fond words convey more poetry to the heart than a whole world of verse.

"We know not any man's history more romantic in its commencement, or more touching in its close, than that of Raleigh—from the first dawn of his fortunes, when he threw his cloak before the foot of royalty, throughout his brilliant rise and long imprisonment, to the hour when royalty rejoiced in his merciless martyrdom.

"Whether the recital of his eloquent speeches, the perusal of his vigorous and original poetry, or the narration of his quaint, yet profound 'History of the World,' engage our attention, all will equally impress us with admiration of his talent, with wonder at his achievements, with sympathy in his misfortunes, and with pity at his fall."

When he was brought upon the scaffold, he felt the edge of the axe with which he was to be beheaded, and observed, "'Tis a sharp remedy, but a sure one for all ills," harangued the people calmly, eloquently, and conclusively, in defence of his character, laid his head on the block with indifference, and died as he had lived, undaunted, one of the greatest benefactors of both England and America, judicially murdered by the pitiful spite of the basest and worst of England's monarchs. James could slay his body, but his fame shall live forever.

> [1] I would here caution my readers from placing the slightest confidence in anything stated in Hume's History (*fable?*) of the Stuarts, and especially of this, the worst of a bad breed.

HOPE ON, HOPE EVER.

BY ROBERT G. ALLISON.

If sorrow's clouds around thee lower,

E'en in affliction's gloomiest hour,

Hope on firmly, hope thou ever;

Let nothing thee from Hope dissever.

What though storms life's sky o'ercast

Time's sorrows will not always last,

This vale of tears will soon be past.

Hope darts a ray to light death's gloom,

And smooths the passage to the tomb;

Hope is to weary mortals given,

To lead them to the joys of heaven

Then, when earth's scenes, however dear,

From thy dim sight shall disappear—

When sinks the pulse, and fails the eye,

Then on Hope's pinions shall thy spirit fly

To fairer worlds above the sky.

Then hope thou on, and hope thou ever;

Let nothing thee from Hope dissever.

THE DRESSING ROOM.

Full bodies not gathered in at the top, but left either quite loose, or so as to form an open fluting, are becoming very fashionable; but they require to be very carefully made, and to have a tight body under them, as otherwise they look untidy—particularly as the age of stiff stays has departed, we trust never to return, and the modern elegants wear stays with very little whalebone in them, if they wear any at all.

In our figures, the one holding the fan has the body of her dress, which is of spotted net, fluted at the top; the skirt is made open at the side, and fastened with a bouquet of roses. The petticoat, which is of pink satin, has a large bow of ribbon with a rose in the centre, just below the rose which fastens the dress. The sleeves are also trimmed with bunches of roses; and the gloves are of a very delicate pale pink.

The other dress is of white net or tarlatan, made with three skirts, and a loose body and sleeves. The upper skirts are both looped up with flowers on the side, and large bows of very pale-yellow ribbon. Ribbon of the same color is worn in the hair, and the gloves are of a delicately tinted yellowish white.

The dress of the standing figure is of rich yellow brocaded silk, trimmed with three flounces of white lace, carried up to the waist, so as to appear like three over skirts, open in front. The body is trimmed with a double berthe of Vandyked lace, which is also carried round the sleeves. The gloves are rather long, and of a delicate cream-color. The hair is dressed somewhat in the Grecian style so as to form a rouleau round the face—the front hair being combed back over a narrow roll of brown silk stuffed with wool, which is fastened round the head like a wreath. A golden bandeau is placed above the rouleau.

The sitting figure shows another mode of arranging the hair. The back hair is curiously twisted, and mixed with narrow rolls of scarlet and white; and the front hair is dressed in waved bandeaux, or it may be curled in what the French call English ringlets. Plain smooth bandeaux have almost entirely disappeared; but bandeaux, with the hair waved, or projecting from the face, are common.

KNITTED FLOWERS.

AMERICAN MARYGOLD.

The prettiest are in *shaded orange*-colored wool (of four threads), which must be split in two, as the Berlin wool. Begin with the darkest shade.

Cast on eight stitches, work them in ribs, four in each row, knitting two stitches; and purling two; both sides must be alike. Continue this till you come to the beginning of the lightest shade; then begin to decrease one stitch at the beginning of every row, till only one stitch remains in the middle; fasten this off, break the wool, and begin the next petal with the darkest shade. Eight petals will be required for each flower. Every petal must be edged with wire; and, in order to do this neatly, you must cover a piece of wire with wool—the middle of the wire with one thread only of brown split wool—and the sides with a lighter shade, to correspond with the color of the petal; sew this round with the same shades of wool.

To make up the flower, it will be necessary to form a tuft of the same shaded wool, *not* split. This is done by cutting five or six bits of wool about an inch long, and placing them across a bit of double wire; twist the wire very tight, and cut the ends of the wool quite even; fasten the eight petals round this, near the top, which can be done either by twisting the wires together or by sewing them round with a rug needle.

CALYX.—The calyx will require four needles.

Cast on twelve stitches, four on each of three needles. Knit in plain rounds till you have about half an inch in length; then knit two stitches in one, break the wool some distance from the work, thread it with a rug needle, and pass the wool behind the little scallop, so as to bring to the next two stitches; work these and the remainder of the stitches in the same manner. Cover a bit of wire with a thread of brown wool, sew it with wool of the same color round the top of the calyx, following carefully the form of the scallops; turn the ends of the wire inside the calyx, and place the flower within it. Tie the calyx under the scallops with a bit of green silk, gather the stitches of the lower part of the calyx with a rug needle and a bit of wool, and cover the stem with split green wool.

Another way of making this flower is by knitting the petals in brioche stitch; but if done thus, nine stitches must be cast on the needle at first, instead of eight, and the flower finished exactly as directed.

BUDS.—The buds are made just in the same manner as the tuft which forms the heart of the flower, only that they must be formed of lighter shades of wool, mixed with a little pale-green wool. The wool must be tightly fixed on the wire by twisting, and then cut very smooth and even. It must be inserted in a small calyx, made as before.

LEAVES.—Each leaf, or small branch, is composed of seven leaflets, of the same size—one at the top, and three on each side; they must be placed in pairs, at a distance of about an inch between each pair.

First leaflet.—Cast on one stitch in a bright, but rather deep shade of yellowish-green wool. Knit and purl alternate rows, increasing one stitch at the beginning of every row till you have seven stitches on the needle; then knit and purl six rows without increase; decrease one stitch at the beginning of the two following rows, and cast off the five remaining stitches. Repeat the same for the six other leaflets. Each leaf must have a fine wire sewn round it, and the stems covered with wool.

CHENILLE WORK

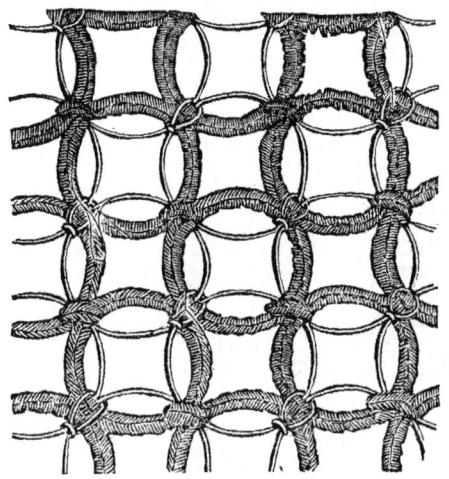

No. 1.—The pattern, full size.

No. 1.—*A new style of Head-Dress. Worked in the second size crimson chenille, with No. 4 gold thread.*

Take a card-board of three inches deep and fifteen inches long, and fasten to the edge of it eleven strands of chenille and gold thread placed together; leave a space of one inch between each strand; the length of the gold and chenille thread must be twenty-four inches. Take the first two threads from the left-hand side, pass the two next under them; tie them in a knot, the two outer over the two centre threads (chenille or gold thread, as may be), and then pass them through the loop formed on the left, and so on till the last row. The shape is an uneven triangle, nine inches from the top corner to the centre, and seven inches from the middle of the front to the centre. When finished, cut off the board, and sew round two sides of the work a fringe of gold thread, which is to fall over the neck.

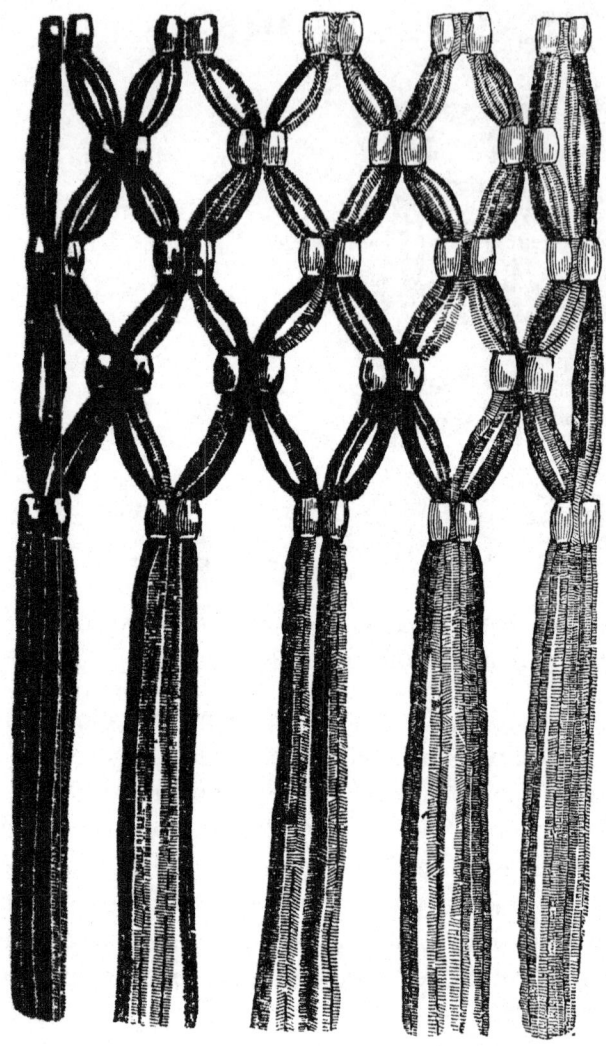

No. 2.—A portion, full size, with fringe.

No. 2.—*Another style of Head-Dress. With white and pink second size chenille.*

This is made nearly in the same manner as No. 1, with chenille, one yard long; but, after having made the first knot, pass a pearl bead on each side, and then make the second knot—the measurement of the meshes to be three-quarters of an inch. When the work is finished, the whole will be twelve inches square. Pass round it an India-rubber cord, which will form the fastening. The ends left from the work to be separately knotted together with silver thread, to hang down, forming a very large and rich tassel.

No. 3.—A portion of the pattern, full size.

No. 3.—*Head-Dress of blue and silver. In chain crochet, silver cord No. 5, with second size of crochet chenille, light blue.*

Eight chain stitches, the last of which is plain crochet, and so on continued. In the two middle stitches of the chenille take up the silver, and in the middle stitches of the silver take up the chenille, each going in a slanting way, once over and once under each other, as the drawing (No. 3) will show. The chenille is worked one way, and the silver goes the other way, contrary to regular crochet work. The whole is worked square, eighteen inches in square; and, when finished, every loop is taken up with fine India-rubber cord, to form the shape. Put round it a silver fringe one inch and a half deep.

CHEMISETTES AND UNDERSLEEVES.

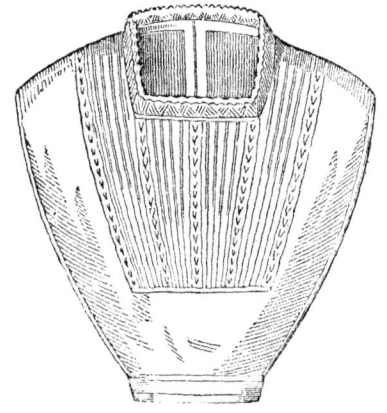

Fig. 1.

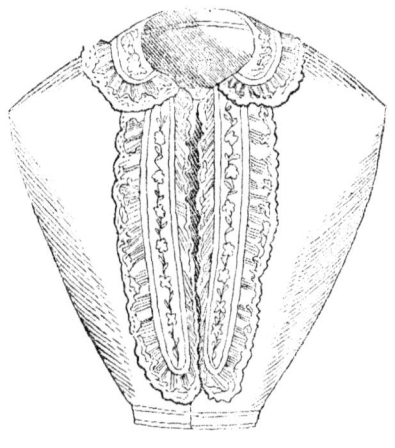

Fig. 2.

All fashionable promenade and evening dresses being cut with an open corsage and loose sleeves, the chemisettes and wristbands become of the greatest importance. There is something very neat in the close coat dress, buttoned up to the throat, and finished only by a cuff at the wrist; but it is never so elegant, after all, as the style now so much in vogue. This season, the V shape from the breast has given place to the square front, introduced from the peasant costumes of France and Italy. It will be seen in fig. 1, which is intended to be worn with that style of corsage, and corresponds to it exactly. The chemisette is composed of alternate rows of narrow plaits and insertion, and is edged with muslin embroidery to correspond. It is decidedly the prettiest and neatest one of the season, and will be found inexpensive.

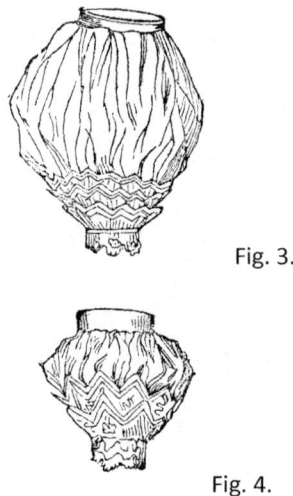

Fig. 3.

Fig. 4.

Fig. 2 has two bands of insertion, surrounded by embroidered muslin frills; the small collar is also edged in the same way. This may be worn with the ordinary V front, or with the square front boddice we have alluded to.

Figs. 3 and 4 are some of the new fashionable undersleeves. It will be noticed that they are very full, and edged with double frills. For further description, see Chit-Chat in December number.

ON A CHILD ASLEEP.

BY JOHN A. CHAPMAN.

See, in that ray of light that child reposes,

Calmly as he a little angel were;

And now and then his eyes he half uncloses,

To see if his bright visions real are.

But what his visions are God only knoweth,

For that sweet child forgets them day by day;

Like breeze of Eden, that so gently bloweth,

They leave no trace when they've passed away.

'Tis thus that innocent childhood ever sleepeth.

With half closed eyes and smiles around its mouth,

At sight of which man's sunken heart upleapeth,

Like chilléd flowers when fanned by the sweet south.

Sleep on, sweet child, smile, as thou sleepest, brightly,

For thou art blest in this thy morning hour;

And, when thou wakest, thou shalt walk more lightly

Than crownéd king, or monarch throned in power.

EDITORS' TABLE.

One perplexing question is settled, viz., that ninety-nine does not make a hundred. Those transcendentally erudite men who contended that the nineteenth century commenced on the 1st of January, 1800, have at last learned to count correctly. So we may venture to affirm, with fear of raising an argument, that this New-Year's Day, 1851, begins the last half of this present century.

Here, then, we stand on the dividing ridge of Time, the topmost pinnacle of humanity; and, looking backward over the vast ocean of life, we can discern amidst the rolling, heaving, struggling surges, which have engulfed so many grand hopes, and towering aims, and strong endeavors during the world's voyage of half a century, that important victories have been won, wonderful things discovered, and great truths brought out of the turmoil in which power, pride, and prejudice were contending fifty years ago. At the beginning of the century, the stirring themes were deeds of war. Now, the palm is won by works of peace. In 1801, the Old World was a battle-field, the centre and moving power of destruction being placed in London. Now, 1851 finds "the whole world kin," as it were, busy in preparing for such an Industrial Convention as was never held since time began: and this, too, centres in London. What trophies of mind and might will be there exhibited! Not victories won by force or fraud, with their advantages appropriated to exalt a few individuals; but real advances made in those arts which give the means of improvement to nations, and add to the knowledge, freedom, and happiness of the people!

We are not intending to enlarge on this theme, which will be better done by abler pens. We only allude to it here, in order to draw the attention of our readers to one curious fact, which those who are aiming to place women in the workshop, to compete with men, should consider: namely, that none, or very few specimens of female ingenuity or industry will be found in the world's great show-shop. The female mind has as yet manifested very little of the kind of genius termed mechanical, or inventive. Nor is it the lack of learning which has caused this uniform lack of constructive talent. Many ignorant men have studied out and made curious inventions of mechanical skill; women never. We are constrained to say we do not believe woman would ever have invented the compass, the printing-press, the steam-engine, or even a loom. The difference between the mental power of the two sexes, as it is distinctly traced in Holy Writ and human history, we have described and illustrated in a work[1] soon to be published. We trust this will prove of importance in settling the question of what woman's province really is, and where her station should be in the onward march of civilization. It is not mechanical, but moral power which is now needed. That woman was endowed with moral goodness superior to that possessed by man is the doctrine of the Bible; and this moral power she must be trained to use for the promotion of goodness, and purity, and holiness in men. There is no need that she should help him in his task of subduing the world. He has the strong arm and the ingenious mind to understand and grapple with things of earth; but he needs her aid in subduing himself, his own selfish passions, and animal propensities.

To sum up the matter, the special gifts of God to men are mechanical ingenuity and physical strength. To women He has given moral insight or instinct, and the patience that endures physical suffering. Both sexes equally need enlightenment of mind or reason by education, in order to make their peculiar gifts of the greatest advantage to themselves, to each other, to the happiness and improvement of society, and to the glory of God.

Such are the principles which we have been striving to disseminate for the last twenty years; and we rejoice, on this jubilee day of the century, that our work has been crowned with good success, and that the prospect before us is bright and cheering. The wise king of Israel asserted the power and predicted the future of woman in these remarkable words, "Strength and honor are her clothing; and she shall rejoice in time to come." And so it will be. But the elevation of the sex will not consist in becoming like man, in doing man's work, or striving for the dominion of the world. The true woman cannot work with materials of earth, build up cities, mould marble forms, or discover new mechanical inventions to aid physical improvement. She has a higher and holier vocation. She works in the elements of human nature; her orders of architecture are formed in the soul. Obedience, temperance, truth, love, piety, these she must build up in the character of her children. Often, too, she is called to repair the ravages and beautify the waste places which sin, care, and the desolating storms of life leave in the mind and heart of the husband she reverences and obeys. This task she should perform faithfully, but with humility, remembering that it was for woman's sake Eden was forfeited, because Adam loved his wife more than his Creator, and that man's nature has to contend with a degree of depravity, or temptation to sin, which the female, by the grace of God, has never experienced. Yes, the wife is dependent on her husband for the position she holds in society; she must rely on him for protection and support; she should look up to him with reverence as her earthly guardian, the "saviour of the body," as St. Paul says, and be obedient. Does any wife say her husband is not worthy of this honor? Then render it to the office with which God has invested him as head of the family; but use your privilege of motherhood so to train your son that he may be worthy of this reverence and obedience from his wife. Thus through your sufferings the world may be made better; every faithful performance of private duty adds to the stock of public virtues.

We trust, before the sands of this century are run out, that these Bible truths will be the rule of faith and of conduct with every American wife and mother, and that the moral influence of American women will be felt and blessed as the saving power not only of our nation, but of the world. Our hopes are high, not only because we believe our principles are true, but because we expect to be sustained and helped by all who are true and right-minded. And this recalls to our thoughts the constant and cheering kindness which has been extended to our periodical during the long period it has been attaining its present wide popularity. We must thank these friends.

[1] "Woman's Record; or Biographical Sketches of all Distinguished Women, from the Creation to the Present Time. Arranged in Four Eras. With Selections from the Female Writers of each Era." The work is now in the press of the Harpers, New York.

TO THE CONDUCTORS OF THE PUBLIC PRESS.

Our Friends Editorial, who, for the last twenty years, have manifested uniform kindness, and always been ready with their generous support, to you, on this jubilee day, we tender our grateful acknowledgments. We have never sought your assistance to us as individuals. Your office should have a higher aim, a worthier estimation. You are guardians of the public welfare, improvement, and progress. Not to favor the success of private speculation, but to promote the dissemination of truths and principles which shall benefit the whole community, makes your glory. We thank you that such has been your course hitherto in regard to the "Lady's Book." The public confidence, which your judicious notices of our work have greatly tended to strengthen, is with us. The chivalry of the American press will ever sustain a periodical devoted to woman; and the warm, earnest, intelligent manner in which you have done this deserves our praise. Like noble and true knights, you have upheld our cause, and we thank you in the name of the thousands of fair and gentle readers of our "Book," to whom we frankly acknowledge that your steady approval has incited our efforts to excel. We invoke your powerful aid to sustain us through the coming years, while we will endeavor to merit your commendations. None know so well as you, our editorial friends, what ceaseless exertions are required to keep the high position we have won. But the new year finds us prepared for a new trial with all literary competitors; and, with the inspiring voice of the public press to cheer us on, we are sure of winning the goal. In the anticipation of this happy result, we wish to all our kind friends—what we enjoy—health, hope, and a HAPPY NEW YEAR.

To CORRESPONDENTS.—The following articles are accepted: "A Dream of the Past," "Sonnet—The God of Day," &c., "My Childhood's Home," "Town and Country Contrasted," "The Artist's Dream," "The Tiny Glove," "The Sisters," and "The Lord's Prayer."

Ellen Moinna's story came too late for the purpose designed. We do not need it.

MANUSCRIPT MUSIC ACCEPTED: "All Around and All Above Thee;" "Oh, Sing that Song again To-Night!" (excellent); "Hope on, Hope Ever;" "The Musing Hour;" "La Gita in Gondola;" "To Mary," by Professor Kehr.

Our friends who send us music must wait patiently for its appearance, *if accepted*. Months must sometimes elapse, as our large edition renders it necessary to print it in advance. Those who wish special answers from our musical editor will please mention the fact in their communications.

EDITORS' BOOK TABLE.

From GEORGE S. APPLETON, corner of Chestnut and Seventh Street, Philadelphia:—

THE POETICAL WORKS OF JOHN MILTON. Edited by Sir Egerton Brydges, Bart. Illustrated with engravings, designed by John Martin and J.W.M. Turner, R.A. We noticed an edition of "Paradise Lost" in our November number. Here, however, we have a complete edition of the modern Homer's works, including "Paradise Regained," and all his minor poems, sonnets, &c. These editions are pleasing testimonials of the renewed interest which the public are beginning to manifest for the writings of standard English authors, in preference to the light and ephemeral productions of those of the present day, who have too long held the classical taste and refinement in obedience to their influences. The illustrations of this edition are very beautiful.

THE COMPLETE WORKS OF ROBERT BURNS; *containing his Poems, Songs, and Correspondence, with a New Life of the Poet, and Notices, Critical and Biographical.* By Allen Cunningham. This edition of the works of the great Scottish poet cannot fail to attract the attention of all who admire the genius and independence of his mind, and of all who wish a full and correct copy of his productions, compiled under the supervision of a man who was himself an excellent poet, and capable of fairly distinguishing the beauties and powers of a poetical mind.

EVERYBODY'S ALMANAC AND DIARY FOR 1851; *containing a List of Government Officers. Commerce and Resources of the Union, Exports of Cotton, and General Information for the Merchant, Tradesman, and Mechanic, together with a Complete Memorandum for every day in the year*. A neat and valuable work.

We have received from the same publisher the following works, compiled for the special benefit of little children and of juvenile learners and readers, all of which are appropriately illustrated:—

LITTLE ANNE'S ABC BOOK.
LITTLE ANNE'S SPELLER.
MOTHER GOOSE. By Dame Goslin.
THE ROSE-BUD. *A Juvenile Keepsake.* By Susan W. Jewett.
GREAT PANORAMA OF PHILADELPHIA. By Van Daube. With twenty-three illustrations.

From HENRY C. BAIRD (successor to E.L. Carey); Philadelphia:—

THE POETICAL WORKS OF THOMAS GRAY. With illustrations by C.W. Radclyffe. Edited, with a memoir, by Henry Reed, Professor of English Literature in the University of Pennsylvania. Great pains have evidently been taken by the editor and the publisher to render this not only the most complete and accurate edition of the works of Gray that has ever been presented to the American public, but also one of the most superbly embellished and beautifully printed volumes of the season, which has called forth so many works intended for presentation.

THE BUILDER'S POCKET COMPANION. This volume contains the elements of building, surveying, and architecture, with practical rules and instructions connected with the subjects, by A.C. Smeaton, Civil Engineer, &c. The inexperienced builder, whether engaged practically, or in the investment of capital in building improvements, will find this to be a very valuable assistant.

THE CABINET-MAKER'S AND UPHOLSTERER'S COMPANION. This work contains much valuable information on the subjects of which it treats, and also a number of useful receipts and explanations of great use to the workmen in those branches. The author, L. Stokes, has evidently taken great pains in the arrangement and compilation of his work.

HOUSEHOLD SURGERY; *or, Hints on Emergencies*. By John F. South, one of the Surgeons to St. Thomas's Hospital. The first American, from the second London edition. A highly valuable book for the family, which does not pretend, however, to supersede the advice and experience of a physician, but merely to have in preparation, and to recommend such remedies as may be necessary until such advice can be obtained. There are many illustrations in the work which will greatly facilitate its practical usefulness.

From LEA & BLANCHARD, Philadelphia:—

THE RACES OF MEN. *A Fragment.* By Robert Knox, M.D., Lecturer on Anatomy, and Corresponding Member of the National Academy of Science in France. The character and tendency of this "fragment," or "outlines of lectures," to use the author's own terms, are such as cannot be suddenly determined upon or understood. This will appear the more evident to the reader from the assurance which he also gives, that his work runs counter to nearly all the chronicles of events called histories; that it shocks the theories of statesmen, theologians, and philanthropists of all shades. He maintains that the human character, individual and national, is traceable solely to the nature of that race to which the individual or nation belongs, which he affirms to be simply a fact, the most remarkable, the most comprehensive which philosophy has announced.

From T. B. PETERSON, 98 Chestnut Street. Philadelphia:—

HORACE TEMPLETON. By Charles Lever. The publisher of this work deserves the thanks of the reading public for presenting it with a cheap edition of so interesting a publication. It has already passed the ordeal of the press, and has been received, both in Europe and in America, as one of the most entertaining productions that has appeared for many years, not excepting "Charles O'Malley," and the other mirth-inspiring volumesof the inimitable Lever.

THE VALLEY FARM; *or, the Autobiography of an Orphan.* Edited by Charles J. Peterson, author of "Cruising in the Last War," &c. A work sound in morals and abounding in natural incident.

RESEARCHES ON THE MOTION OF THE JUICES IN THE ANIMAL BODY, AND THE EFFECTS OF EVAPORATIONS IN PLANTS; *together with an Account of the Origin of the Potatoe Disease, with full and Ingenious Directions for the Protection and Entire Prevention of the Potatoe Plant against all Diseases.* By Justus Liebig, M.D., Professor of Chemistry in the University of Giessen; and edited from the manuscript of the author, by William Gregory, M.D., of the University of Edinburgh. A valuable treatise, as its title sufficiently indicates.

From PHILLIPS, SAMPSON & Co., Boston, through T.B. PETERSON, Philadelphia:—

A PEEP AT THE PILGRIMS IN SIXTEEN HUNDRED AND THIRTY-SIX. *A Tale of Olden Times.* By Mrs. H.V. Cheney. Those who feel an interest in the records and monuments of the past, and who desire to study the characteristics of the Pilgrim Fathers, and Pilgrim Mothers and Daughters, will not fail to avail themselves of the graphic delineations presented to them in this entertaining volume.

SHAKSPEARE'S DRAMATIC WORKS. No. 25. Containing "Troilus and Cressida," with a very fine engraving.

From JOHN S. TAYLOR, New York, through T.B. PETERSON, Philadelphia:—

LETTERS FROM THE BACKWOODS AND THE ADIRONDAC. By the Rev. J.T. Headley. Also,

THE POWER OF BEAUTY. By the same author. Illustrated editions.

From LINDSAY & BLAKISTON, Philadelphia:—

MOSAIQUE FRANCAISE: *ou Choix De Sujets Anecdotiques, Historiques, Littéraires et Scientifiques, tirés pour La Plupart D'Auteurs Modernes.* Par F. Séron, Homme de lettres, l'un des rédacteurs du Journal Française; Les Monde des enfans, Revue Encyclopédique de la jeunesse de 1844 à 1848, etc.; Professeur de Langue et de Littérature Française à Philadelphie.

This work appears to have been compiled with great care, from works by the best French authors. Every subject has been carefully excluded that could in any manner wound or bias the preconceived opinions of the American reader in relation to religious or political freedom.

From HARPER & BROTHERS, New York, through LINDSAY & BLAKISTON, Philadelphia:—

MEMOIRS OF THE LIFE AND WRITINGS OF THOMAS CHALMERS, D.D., LL.D. By his son-in-law, the Rev. Wm. Hanna, LL.D. The appearance of the second volume of these memoirs will be hailed with pleasure by the admirers of Dr. Chalmers, whose reputation as a Christian minister, and as a writer of extraordinary beauty and power, has long preceded these volumes.

GENEVIEVE; *or, the History of a Servant Girl*. Translated from the French of Alphonse de Lamartine. By A.A. Seoble.

ADDITIONAL MEMOIRS OF MY LIFE. By A. De Lamartine.

THE PICTORIAL FIELD BOOK OF THE REVOLUTION. No. 8. This excellent and patriotic work fully sustains the spirit and interest that marked its commencement.

From the PROTESTANT EPISCOPAL SUNDAY SCHOOL UNION, New York, through A. HART, Philadelphia:—

THE OLD MAN'S HOME. By the Rev. William Adams, M.A., author of the "Shadow of the Cross," &c. With engravings, from designs by Weir. Sixth American edition. An affecting tale, written in a familiar style, and peculiarly calculated to impress upon the youthful mind the importance of those moral and religious truths which it is the aim of the author to inculcate.

From GOULD, KENDALL & LINCOLN, Boston, through DANIELS & SMITH, Philadelphia:—

THE PRE-ADAMITE EARTH: *Contributions to Theological Science*. By John Harris, D.D., author of "The Great Teacher," &c. The present volume is the "third thousand," which we presume to mean the "third edition," revised and corrected, of this work, which may be considered a successful effort to reconcile the dogmas of theology with the progress of philosophy and science. The style of the author is argumentative and eloquent, evincing great knowledge and zeal in the development of the interesting subjects connected with his treatise.

RELIGIOUS PROGRESS: *Discourses on the Development of the Christian Character*. By William R. Williams. Comprising five lectures originally prepared for the pulpit, and delivered by their author to the people under his charge. These lectures are chaste and graceful in style, and sound and vigorous in argument.

From TICKNOR, REED & FIELDS, Boston.

BIOGRAPHICAL ESSAYS. By Thomas De Quincey, author of "Confessions of an English Opium Eater," etc. This is the second volume of Mr. De Quincey's writings, now in course of publication. It contains biographical sketches of Shakspeare, Pope, Charles Lamb, Goethe, and Schiller, accompanied by numerous notes, which, with the author's acknowledged taste, will give a new interest to these almost familiar subjects.

ASTRÆA. *The Balance of Illusions.* A poem delivered before the Phi Beta Kappa Society of Yale College, August 14, 1850, by Oliver Wendell Holmes. This poem contains many beautiful gems, interspersed with some satirical descriptions of men and manners, which prove Mr. Holmes to be a caustic as well as an amusing writer.

NEW MUSIC.

We have received from Mr. Oliver Diston, No. 115 Washington Street, Boston, a collection of beautiful music, got up in his usual taste.

The Prima Donna Polka. By Edward L. White.

The German Schottisch. By T.S. Lloyd. And

The Starlight Polka. Three excellent polkas, with music enough in them to draw the proper steps from every heel and toe in the land.

Oh, Come to the Ingleside! A sweet ballad by Eliza Cook, the music by W.H. Aldridge.

A Mother's Prayer.. By J.E. Gould.

The Araby Maid. By J.T. Surenne.

Old Ironsides at Anchor lay. One of Dodge's favorite songs, the words by Morris, the music by B. Covert.

A Little Word. By Niciola Olivieri (!).

The Parting Look. Words by Henry Sinclair, music by Alex. Wilson. Embellished by a fine lithograph.

The Dying Boy. Another of Dodge's favorite songs. The words are by Mrs. Larned, and the music by Lyman Heath. This song has also a fine engraving.

Mr. Diston has also commenced the publication of Beethoven's Sonatas for the piano forte, from the newly revised edition, published by subscription in Germany.

MESSRS. LEE & WALKER, No. 162 Chestnut Street, Philadelphia, are now publishing "*Lindiana*," a choice selection of Jenny Lind's songs, with brilliant variations by the untiring Chas. Grobe. The first is the "Dream." In the hands of Professor Grobe, we cannot doubt the entire success of the enterprise. The series is dedicated to "our musical editor," who fully appreciates the compliment and returns his sincere thanks.

Our old friend Mr. James Conenhoven, associated with Mr. Duffy, has opened a new music store at No. 120 Walnut Street, Philadelphia. From Mr. C.'s known taste and knowledge of the business, we anticipate his entire success, and cheerfully recommend our friends to make his early acquaintance in his new career. They have sent us the *Silver Bell Waltz*, by Mr. Conenhoven himself, and *Solitude*, a beautiful song by Kirk White, the music by John Daniel. Both are very handsomely got up, and are valuable accessions to a musical portfolio.

OUR TITLE-PAGE.—Those who are fond of Fashions other than colored will be gratified with our title-page, which contains at least fifty figures.

PRINTING IN COLORS.—We give another specimen in this number, of printing in colors from a STEEL plate. We believe that we have the only artisans in this country that can do this kind of fancy work. The present specimen, which we are willing to contrast with any other plate in any magazine for this month, is entirely of American manufacture.

We will send a copy of the November and December numbers of the Lady's Book, containing the Lord's Prayer and the Creed, gratis, to any religious publication with which we do not exchange, if it will signify a wish to have them.

NEW-YEAR'S DAY IN FRANCE.—All who have visited this gay country at the season of the holidays, will be struck with the graphic power displayed by our artist in the plate that graces the present number.

ORIGINAL DESIGNS.—The four principal plates in this number, viz., The Constant, The Four Eras of Life, The Four Seasons, and The Double Fashion Plate, as well as several of the wood engravings, are from original designs. This originality has never before been attempted in any magazine of any country. We do not remember an instance of the kind in any of the English annuals. It is our intention to be ever progressive. Our original designs last year were numerous: among them the never-to-be-forgotten Lord's Prayer and Creed. "The Coquette," the match plate to "The Constant," will appear in the March number. It will be seen by this number that we are able to transcend anything we have yet presented. Our Book, this year, shall be one continuous triumph. As we have only ourselves for a rival, our effort will be to excel even the well-known versatility and beauty which our Book has always exhibited.

PROFESSOR BLUMENTHAL.—We omitted to include among our list of contributors this gentleman's name. It was an oversight; but the professor shows, by his article in this number, that he has not forgotten us.

ARTHUR'S STORY.—With but one exception, Mr. Arthur writes for his own paper alone. The story in this number will amply repay a careful perusal. It will be completed in the March number.

T. S. ARTHUR'S HOME GAZETTE.—In our acquaintance with newspaperdom, as Willis would say, which extends over a period of twenty-two years, the history of this paper is the most singular of any in our recollection. Ample capital was provided to meet any exigency that might arise; but, strange to say, not a penny of it has been used. But we were too hasty; for, when we consider who is its editor, it must be confessed it is *not* strange. The paper has paid for itself from the start. Perhaps another instance of the kind lives not in the memory of that well-known person, "the oldest inhabitant." Mr. Arthur now counts his subscribers by thousands, nearly by tens of thousands. The rush for it has been unexampled—so much so as to make it necessary to reprint early numbers, and even to telegraph for extra supplies of paper, so rapidly has it been exhausted. Mr. Arthur has struck a vein that will render a voyage to California entirely useless to him. His advertisement will be found in this number.

We will mention one fact, and our subscribers will see the remon of it. We give no preference as regards the first impressions from the plates. If a plate wears in the printing, we have it retouched, so that all may have impressions alike. With our immense edition, the greatest ever known, this we find sometimes necessary.

On reference to our advertisement in this number, it will be seen what is in store for the subscribers to Godey. When we announce the fact that the plates are engraved in the same style as those they have seen, "The Lord's Prayer," "The Evening Star," "The Creed," "We Praise Thee, O God," and those contained in the present number, they will conclude that a rich treat is to be obtained for the trifling outlay of $3. Would it not be a convenient method, where it is difficult to obtain a club of five subscribers, to remit us $10 for a club of five years? Any person remitting $10 in advance, will be entitled to the Lady's Book five years. We cannot forbear inserting the following notices:—

"The Lady's Book is the best, most sociable, and decidedly the richest magazine for truth, virtue, and literary worth now published in this country."—*Indiana Gazette.*

"In matter of sentiment, and light literature, and elegant embellishments of useful and ornamental art, Godey's Lady's Book takes the lead of all works of its class. We have seen nothing in it offensive to the most fastidious taste."—*Church Quarterly Review and Ecclesiastical Reporter*.

"We find it difficult, without resorting to what would be thought downright hyperbole, to express adequately the admiration excited by the appearance of this last miracle of literary and artistic achievement."—*Maine Gospel Banner.*

The above are unsolicited opinions from grave authorities.

NEW MATTER FOR THE WORK TABLE.—The ladies will perceive that they have been well cared for in this number. We again give, for their benefit, two new styles of work, "The Chenille Work," and "Knitted Flowers".

THE HAIR WORK will be continued in our next number.

BLITZ HAS ARRIVED.—What joy this will carry into the minds of the young! Blitz, the conjurer, the kind-hearted Blitz, who dispenses his sugar things amongst his young friends with such a smile—and they are real sugar things, too; they don't slip through your fingers, except in the direction of your mouth, like many of the things he gives the young folks to hold—is at his old quarters, the Lecture-room at the Museum.

A.B. WARDEN, at his jewelry and silver ware establishment, S.E. corner of Fifth and Chestnut streets, has an immense variety of beautiful and valuable presents for the season. He is the sole agent for a new style of watch lately introduced into this country, approved by the Chronometer Board at the Admiralty, in London, which is warranted. Orders by mail, including a description of the desired article, will be attended to.

The Weber Minstrels is the title assumed by some gentlemen of this city, who intend to give concerts here and elsewhere. We commend them to our friends of the press in the various places they may visit. We can speak confidently of their singing; and we are sure that, wherever they go, their manners as gentlemen and their talent as singers will commend them to public favor.

FROM OUR MUSICAL EDITOR.

BERKSHIRE HOTEL, *Pittsfield, Mass.*,

Sept. 22, 1850.

MY DEAR GODEY.—You know I do not often *brag* of *Hotels*, and it is perhaps out of the line of the "Book." But, in this particular instance, I know you will excuse me, when I write of a spot in which you would delight. I wish, in the first place, to introduce you to MR. W.B. COOLEY, the perfect pink of landlords, wearing a polka cravat and a buff vest, externally; but he has a heart in his bosom as big as one of the Berkshire cattle. If you ever come here—and by *you*, I mean the 100,000 subscribers to the Lady's Book, don't go anywhere else, for *here* you will find a home—a regular New England *home*. His table is magnificent—his beds and rooms all that any one could ask; and his friendly nature will make you perfectly *at home*. Indeed, it is the only hotel I have been at, on my protracted tour, where I have felt perfectly *at home*.

How I wish you, and your wife and daughters, and lots of our mutual friends, were here with me. We would have glorious times—music, dancing, singing, sight-seeing, conversation, &c. &c. I cannot write much; but I wish you to understand that this is the *ne plus ultra* of hotels. Don't fail to patronize it. Lebanon Springs and the Shaker settlement are within a short ride.

Yours ever,
J.C.

VARIOUS USEFUL RECEIPTS, &c., OF OUR OWN GATHERING.

Rice for curry should never be immersed in water, except that which has been used for cleaning the grain previous to use. It should be placed in a sieve and heated by the steam arising from boiling water; the sieve so placed in the saucepan as to be two or three inches above the fluid. In stirring the rice a light hand should be used, or you are apt to amalgamate the grains; the criterion of well-dressed rice being to have the grains separate.

ARROW-ROOT FOR INVALIDS.—The practice of boiling arrow-root in milk is at once wasteful and unsatisfactory; the best mode of preparing enough for an invalid's supper is as follows: Put a dessertspoonful of powder, two lumps of sugar, into a chocolate cup, with a few drops of Malaga, or any other sweet wine; mix these well together, and add, in small quantities, more wine, until a smooth thick paste is formed. Pour boiling water, by slow degrees, stirring all the while, close to the fire, until the mixture becomes perfectly transparent.

CUSTARD OR SPONGE-CAKE PUDDING, WITH FRUIT SAUCE.—Break separately and clear in the usual way[1] four large or five small fresh eggs, whisk them until they are light, then throw in a very small pinch of salt, and two tablespoonfuls of pounded sugar; then whisk them anew until it is dissolved: add to them a pint of new milk and a slight flavoring of lemon, orange-flower water, or aught else that may be preferred. Pour the mixture into a plain well buttered mould or basin, and tie securely over it a buttered paper and a small square of cloth or muslin rather thickly floured. Set it into a saucepan or stewpan containing about two inches in depth of boiling water, and boil the pudding very gently for half an hour and five minutes at the utmost. It must be taken out directly it is done, but should remain several minutes before it is dished, and will retain its heat sufficiently if not turned out for ten minutes or more. Great care must always be taken to prevent either the writing paper or the cloth tied over the pudding from touching the water when it is steamed in the manner directed above, a method which is preferable to boiling, if the preceding directions be attended to, particularly for puddings of this class. The corners of the cloth or muslin should be gathered up and fastened over the pudding; but neither a large nor a heavy cloth should be used for the purpose at any time. Three or four sponge biscuits may be broken into the basin before the custard is put in; it must then stand for twenty minutes or half an hour, to soak them, previously to being placed in a saucepan. The same ingredients will make an excellent pudding, *if very slowly baked* for about three quarters of an hour. Four eggs will then be quite sufficient for it.

> [1] That is to say, remove the specks with the point of a fork from each egg while it is in the cup; but if this cannot be adroitly done, so as to clear them off perfectly, whisk up the eggs until they are as liquid as they will become, and then pass them through a hair sieve: after this is done, whisk them afresh, and add the sugar to them.

By particular request we again publish the following receipt:—

NEW RECEIPT FOR A WASHING MIXTURE.

BY MISS LESLIE.

Take two pounds of the best brown soap; cut it up and put it in a clean pot, adding one quart of clean soft water. Set it over the fire and melt it thoroughly, occasionally stirring it up from the bottom. Then take it off the fire, and stir in one tablespoonful of *real* white wine vinegar; two large tablespoonfuls of hartshorn spirits; and seven large tablespoonfuls of spirits of turpentine. Having stirred the ingredients well together, put up the mixture *immediately* into a stone jar, and cover it immediately, lest the hartshorn should evaporate. Keep it always carefully closely covered. When going to wash, nearly fill a six or eight gallon tub with soft water, as hot as you can bear your hand in it, and stir in two large tablespoonfuls of the above mixture. Put in as many white clothes as the water will cover. Let them soak about an hour, moving them about in the water occasionally. It will only be necessary to rub with your hands such parts as are very dirty; for instance, the inside of shirt collars and wristbands, &c. The common dirt will soak out by means of the mixture. Wring the clothes out of the suds, and rinse them well through *two* cold waters.

Next put into a wash kettle sufficient water to boil the clothes (it must be cold at first), and add to it two more tablespoonfuls of the mixture. Put in the clothes after the mixture is well stirred into the water, and boil them *half an hour* at the utmost, not more. Then take them out and throw them into a tub of cold water. Rinse them well through this; and lastly, put them into a second tub of rinsing water, slightly blued with the indigo bag.

Be very careful to rinse them in *two* cold waters out of the first suds, and after the boiling; then wring them and hang them out.

This way of washing with the soap mixture saves much labor in rubbing; expedites the business, and renders the clothes very white, without injuring them in the least. Try it.

DESCRIPTION OF STEEL FASHION PLATE.

We challenge comparison in the design and execution, to say nothing of the accuracy, of our fashion plate. The first is as pretty a home scene as one could wish, and the costumes are brought in naturally. For instance, the promenade dress of the visitor, *Fig. 1st.* A plain stone-colored merino, with green turc satin, a coat or martle made to fit close to the figure, with sleeves demi-width. The trimming is not a simple quilting, like that worn the past season, as it would at first appear, but an entirely new style of silk braid put on in basket-work. Drawn bonnet of apple-green satin, lined with pink, and, with a small muff, the dress is complete.

Fig. 2d is a morning-dress, that would be very pretty to copy for a bridal wardrobe. In the engraving, it is represented of pink silk, with an open corsage, and sleeves demi-long. The chemisette is of lace, to match that upon the skirt, and is fastened at the throat by a simple knot of pink ribbon. The trimming of the dress is quilled ribbon, and the cap has a band and knot of the same color.

Fig. 3d is a mourning costume of silk, with four rows of heavily-knotted fringe upon the skirt, and the sleeves trimmed to correspond. The figures of the children are simple and easily understood. The pelisse of the little girl has an edge to correspond with the muff.

In the second and out-door scene, the artist has very happily given us a glimpse of sleigh-riding in the city. The pedestrians are tastefully dressed, the first figure having one of the most graceful cloaks of the season; it is of stone-colored Thibet cloth, and is trimmed with a fold of the same corded with satin. The sleeves are peculiar, and deserve particular attention. The bonnet is of uncut velvet, with satin bands.

The dress of the second figure will be found very comfortable. It is of thick Mantua silk; trimmed heavily down the entire front breadth. The sacque, of the same, is lined with quilted white satin, as are the loose open sleeves. The sleeves of the dress open in a point at the wrist, to display the undersleeves. The bonnet is a pink casing, with bouquet of roses.

CHIT-CHAT UPON PHILADELPHIA FASHIONS FOR JANUARY.

EVENING DRESS.—Of all the uncomfortable sensations one can experience in society, that of being over or *under*-dressed is the most uncomfortable. It fetters your movements, it distracts your thoughts, and makes conversation next to impossible, unless you have an extraordinary degree of moral courage. We can speak from experience, and so can any of our lady readers, we venture to say.

"Come early; there won't be more than half a dozen people," says your friend, as she flies out of your room at the hotel, after having given you notice that a few of her intimates are to meet you that evening at her house. Take her at her word, of course. Go at half past seven, and ten to one the gas will not be turned on, and your hostess is still at her toilet. Presently, in she sails, making a thousand apologies at having been detained, and is so glad that you have kept your promise and come early. You look at her elaborate toilet, and think your old friend has become extravagantly fond of dress if this is her reception of half a dozen people. An hour, almost an hour by the marble time-piece, drags on. Not a visitor appears. At length, you are refreshed by a faint tinkle of the door bell. A lady shortly enters, saying, "Don't think me a Goth for coming so early." After she is introduced to you, a stolen glance at the clock. Early! It is half-past eight. What time do they intend to come? But now they arrive faster and faster, and each more elaborately dressed than the last, it seems to your startled eyes. A triple lace skirt glides in. You look at your dark green cashmere in dismay. Low neck and short sleeves! Yours is up to the throat. But you mentally thank your mantua-maker for inserting undersleeves; they are quite consoling. Dozens of white kid gloves! You have not even mitts, and your hand is fairly red with the same blush that suffuses your face. In fine, it is an actual party, dancing, supper, and all, given to you; and yet there you sit, among entire strangers dumb from annoyance, and awkward for the first time in many years, perhaps.

But you will not be caught so again. You are wiser from fearful experience. A similar invitation is met with an appeal to your very best party dress, and you go armed *cap-à-pie*, even to white satin slippers. The clock strikes nine as you enter the room, and there is your truth-loving hostess, with her half dozen plain guests, who had given you up, and are sorry you cannot stay long, "as they see you are dressed for a party." Capital suggestion! Make the most of it, and retire as soon as possible under that plea.

We appeal to you, ladies, whether this is a fancy sketch; and yet sometimes it is not the fault of the hostess—you really do not know how you are expected to arrange your toilet. It is to obviate this evil that we propose giving a few plain hints on evening dress.

We once knew a very nice lady, who had come to town for the purpose of taking music lessons. She was entirely unfamiliar with the etiquette of the toilet, and living at a boarding house, there was no one she felt at entire liberty to consult. A gentleman invited her to the opera. She was wild with delight. It was a cold winter's night, and she dressed accordingly. She wore a dark merino dress and cloak, a heavy velvet bonnet and plumes, and thick knit gloves, dark also. The gentleman looked astonished, but said nothing; and imagine her consternation, when she found herself in the centre of the dress circle, in the midst of unveiled necks and arms, thin white dresses, and white kid gloves. At once the oddity of her mistake flashed across her; but she bore it with unparalleled firmness, and enjoyed the music notwithstanding. The lorgnettes attracted by her costume, found a very sweet face to repay them, and her naive and enthusiastic criticism interested her companion so much that he forgot all else.

And how should she have dressed? Cloaks—and what is an opera toilet without a cloak?—are nothing more than sacques of bright cashmere or velvet, lined with quilted silk or satin, with loose flowing sleeves. A shawl is, of course, thrown over this out of doors. One of the prettiest cloaks of this season was made by Miss Wharton, of black satin, with a hood lined with Pompadour pink. But cashmere is less expensive, and may be trimmed with pointed silk or satin, and lined with the same colored silk. Your dress is not of so much consequence, if it is light, for the cloak conceals it. But the undersleeves should be very nice, and white kid gloves are indispensable. A scarf or hood may be worn to the door of the box, and then thrown over the arm. The hair is dressed with very little ornament this winter; but, whatever the head-dress adopted, the two chief points are simplicity and *becomingness*. Dress hats are allowed; but, as they obstruct the view of others, are not desirable.

Nearly the same dress is proper for a subscription concert, where you are sure of a large audience; of course, where Jenny Lind is the attraction, the same thing is certain. All her concerts are *dress* concerts. But, for a ballad *soirée*, or the first appearance of any new star, a pretty hat, with an opera cloak or light shawl, is quite sufficient. For panoramas, negro minstrels, or evening lectures, an ordinary walking costume is sufficient, and it would be very bad taste to go with the head uncovered.

A party dress should be regulated by the invitation, in a measure. In "sociables," the most sensible of all parties, a light silk, mousseline, or cashmere, is sufficient, with short sleeves and a pretty collar. Gloves are by no means indispensable, and many prefer black silk mitts. If the number of invitations exceeds twenty-five, a regular evening dress is expected, as well as at weddings, receptions, or a dancing party. A full evening costume we have often described, and shall give some new styles next month.

Of course, we have spoken only of young ladies, a more matronly style being expected from their chaperons. For instance, caps at the opera or concerts, a charming variety of which were seen at Miss

Wilson's November opening. Turc satins, velvets, and brocades are to those in place of white tulle or embroidered crepes. And again, our hints of course are intended for the city alone, and for the guidance of those who are making that perilous venture, a "first winter in society."

FASHION.

THE BOOK OF THE NATION.

GODEY'S LADY'S BOOK FOR 1851,

LITERARY AND PICTORIAL,

DEVOTED TO AMERICAN ENTERPRISE, AMERICAN WRITERS, AND AMERICAN ARTISTS.

The publisher of the Lady's Book having the ability, as well as the inclination, to make the best monthly literary, and pictorial periodical in this country, is determined to show the patrons of magazines to what perfection this branch of literature can be brought. He has now been publishing the Lady's Book for twenty-six years and he appeals to his subscribers and the public whether the "Book" has not improved every year, and he now pledges his well-earned reputation that, in the MORALITY and SUPERIORITY of his literature, and in the PURITY and BEAUTY of his engravings,

THE LADY'S BOOK FOR 1851 SHALL EXCEED EVERY OTHER MAGAZINE.

The literary department will still be conducted by

MRS. SARAH J. HALE,

whose name is now recognized throughout our country as the able champion of her sex in all that pertains to the proper rights of woman. Arrangements have been made with other than our well known contributors, and we shall have the pleasure of adding to the following some writers of great celebrity, whose names have not yet appeared in the "Book."

Mrs. J.C. Neal,

Mrs. E.F. Ellet,

Enna Duval,

Mrs. E. Oakes Smith,

Mrs. A.F. Law,

The Author of Miss Bremer's Visit to Cooper's Landing,

Mrs. L.G. Abell,

Mrs. O.M.P. Lord,

Kate Berry,

Mrs. S.J. Hale,

F.E.F.,

Mary Spenser Pease,

The Author of "Aunt Magwire,"

Mrs. C.F. Orne,

Mrs. J.H. Campbell,

W. Gilmore Simms,

H.T. Tuckerman,

Park Benjamin,

Hon. R.T. Conrad,

John Neal,

Tom Owen (the Bee Hunter),

Alfred B. Street,

George P. Morris,

Rev. H.H. Weld,

H. Wm. Herbert,

Professor Wm. Alexander,

Professor Alden,

Professor John Frost,

T.S. Arthur,

Richard Coe,

Herman Melville,

Nathl. Hawthorn,

and a host of other names, which our space will not permit us to mention. In short, no efforts will be wanting to retain for Godey's Lady's Book the proud title of

THE LEADING PERIODICAL IN AMERICA.

It will be seen that we have commenced furnishing original designs for our

MODEL COTTAGE

department, than which no set of illustrations have ever given more satisfaction.

THE LADIES' DEPARTMENT

is one that we particularly pride ourselves upon. We have been the first to give everything new in this line—Crochet Work, Knitting, Netting, Patch Work, Crochet Flower Work, Leather Work, Hair Braiding, Ribbon Work, Chenille Work, Lace Collar Work, D'Oyley Watch Safes, Children's and Infants' Clothes, Caps, Capes, Chemisettes, and, in fact, everything that we thought would please our readers. In addition, we have also commenced the publication of

UNDOUBTED RECEIPTS

for Cooking, Removing Stains, and every matter that can interest the head of a family.

GODEY'S RELIABLE FASHION PLATES.

This department will be under the sole superintendence of a lady—one of our first modistes—who receives proof sheets of the fashions direct from Paris, and is intimately connected with the publishers in that city. This favor is granted to her exclusively. They are arranged, under her direction, to suit the more subdued taste of American ladies. There is no other magazine in America that can be equally favored. We have so long led in this department that the fact would hardly be worth mentioning, excepting that others claim the merit that has so long been conceded to the "Book." They will be got up, as usual, in our superior style to the French.

NEW MUSIC, PRINTED SEPARATE

on tinted paper. This is another advantage that Godey possesses over all others. A gentleman is engaged expressly to attend to this department, and no music is inserted in the "Book" that has not undergone his strict supervision.

ILLUSTRATIONS.

In artistic merit, the "Book" will still retain its pre-eminence, and, in order to show the public wherein our superiority will consist, we give the titles of some of the plates that we have now on hand ready for use, all of which will be given in succession. It will be observed that we have, in a measure, quit the beaten track of copying from engravings, as most of our plates are from original designs, prepared expressly for the "Book," by

CROOME, ROTHERMEL, TUCKER, PEASE, DALLAS, PETERS, & GILBERT.

Those that are not from original designs, prepared expressly for us, are from the original painting. Furthermore, the publisher of the "Book" would state that they are ALL STEEL PLATES, and that there is not a WOOD-CUT amongst them. We will not deceive by publishing a list of plates without, at the same time stating whether they are engraved on wood or steel.

It may as well be also stated that Mr. Tucker, our own artist, than whom no one stands higher in America, has been in London for more than a year, and all his plates are now finished. One series of our plates in line engraving will be

CONSTANCY AND COQUETRY,

done in a style to defy any imitation in mezzotint,

GOOD COUNSEL AND EVIL COUNSEL,

DRESS THE MAKER AND DRESS THE WEARER

THE VALENTINES.

The fires of February lit the hearth,

And shone with welcome lustre on the brows

Of two most lovely maidens, as they sat

Expecting, in their heart of hearts, the notes

Called "*Valentines*," that February brings

Upon its fourteenth day, to tell, in rhyme,

All fair and gentle ladies whether they

Have made new conquests, or have kept the old

As fresh as new-blown roses in the hearts

Of their admiring slaves. One of the girls

(Laughing and lovely was she), ever won

High hearts to do her bidding, dreaming it

No sin that *all* should yield her love and homage,

Yet was no trifling, passionless coquette.

Her winning beauty was the standing toast

Of the wide neighborhood, and serenades

From many a gallant woke the sleeping echoes

Beneath her window, and her name was like

The silvery pealing of a tinkling bell;

(Perhaps 'tis yours, fair reader,) "Clairinelle."

May sat beside her with a graver air,

Something more matronly controlled her mien;

Yet was she not a sighing "sentimentalist,"

But, like her cousin Cary, could be gay:

Two Valentines had come for these fair girls,

Which made the dimpled smiles show teeth like pearls

Pray, read those tender missives—here they are—

CLAIRINELLE'S VALENTINE.

The maiden I love is the fairest on earth,

Her laugh is the clear, joyous music of mirth;

I think of the angels whenever she sings—

She's a seraph from Heaven, but folding her wings.

The least little act that she doeth is kind;

Her goodness all springs from a beautiful mind.

I love her much more than I know how to tell;

Let her do what she will, it is always done well:

Her voice is the murmur the mild zephyr makes

As it steals through the forest and ruffles the lakes:

Her eyes are so gentle, so calm, and so blue,

That I'm sure that she's constant, and trusting, and true:

Her features are delicate, classic, and pure:

Her hair is light chestnut, and I'm almost sure

That the sunbeams that bathe it can't set themselves free:

Her teeth are like pearls from the depths of the sea.

A bee in a frolic once stung her red lip,

And left there the honey he hastened to sip:

Let her go where she will, she is always the belle,

And her name, her sweet name, is the fair Clairinelle.

MAY'S VALENTINE.

MY UNSENTIMENTAL COUSIN:—

The moon was half bewildered by the vexing clouds

That did beset her in her path serene,

Veiling her beauty with their envious shrouds,

Hiding her glorious, most majestic mien.

There was a depth of silence in the night—

A mist of melancholy in the air—

And the capricious beams of Dian's light

Gave something mystic to the scene most fair.

I gave my cousin Dante's divine "Inferno,"

Imploring her to read *il primo canto*.

"Lo giorno s'andava," she drawled; but, tired of plodding,

Directly fell asleep, and pretty soon—*was nodding*!!

"Cousin, sweet cousin," cried I out, "awake!

I long for sympathy—compassion on me take:

They say yon stars are worlds—dost think 'tis so?"

"Really, my—dear (*a yawn*), I—don't exactly know."

"Cousin," said I, "upon a night like this,

Back to the heart steal distant memories

From out the vista of the waning past"—

"Harry, I've caught the horrid fly at last!"

Shades of the angry Muses! worse and worse!

She disappears!—is gone!—*to knit a crochet purse*!!

"Cousin, come back again!" in vain I cried;

Echo (the mocking-bird!) *alone* replied.

CARA.

CORNERS FOR POCKET HANDKERCHIEFS.

BIRTHDAY OF THE YEAR

Timeless books such as:

FOR KIDS, PARTNERS AND FRIENDS

Alice in Wonderland • The Jungle Book • The Wonderful Wizard of Oz
Peter and Wendy • Robin Hood • The Prince and The Pauper
The Railway Children • Treasure Island • A Christmas Carol

Adults

Romeo and Juliet • Dracula

Visit Im TheStory.com *and order yours today!*

Printed in Dunstable, United Kingdom